In the Green Kitchen

In the Green Kitchen

Techniques to Learn by Heart

Alice Waters

— ⤜⤛ —

PHOTOGRAPHS BY
HIRSHEIMER & HAMILTON

CLARKSON POTTER / PUBLISHERS
NEW YORK

All rights reserved.
Published in the United States by
ClarksonPotter/Publishers, an imprint of the Crown
Publishing Group, a division of Random House, Inc.,
New York.
www.crownpublishing.com
www.clarksonpotter.com

CLARKSON POTTER is a trademark and POTTER with colophon
is a registered trademark of Random House, Inc.

Library of Congress Cataloging-in-Publication Data
is available upon request.

ISBN 978-0-307-33680-4

Printed in the United States of America

Design by Patricia Curtan

10   9   8   7   6   5   4   3   2   1

First Edition

Proceeds from *In the Green Kitchen* will benefit the Chez Panisse Foundation in support of Edible Education—a national movement to change the way children eat and how they learn about food in the public schools. The Edible Schoolyard in Berkeley, California, is a hopeful and nourishing curriculum that engages all children in the growing of a garden, in the cooking of food, and in the pleasure of the table. This book is dedicated to the students of Martin Luther King Middle School.

« Contents »

« WHAT IS THE GREEN KITCHEN? »

The Green Kitchen began at a large, joyous gathering in San Francisco that attracted thousands of cooks and eaters, farmers and ranchers, cheese makers and winemakers, bakers and beekeepers, fishermen and foragers—all united by a passion for food and for a sustainable future. I was lucky enough to be one of the organizers of this event, which was called Slow Food Nation. We knew people were coming from all over the country to taste and learn, so we decided to include a demonstration kitchen to show what all good cooks have in common: a set of basic techniques that are universal to all cuisines. Once learned by heart, these are the techniques that free cooks from an overdependence on recipes and a fear of improvisation.

The basic techniques of good cooking do not require a lavish kitchen or a lot of specialized equipment. Far from it: For our demonstration kitchen at Slow Food Nation, all we had was a table, a couple of sharp knives and a cutting board, a hot plate and a few pots, a mortar and pestle, and a compost bucket. We called it the Green Kitchen, and we invited a diverse group of well-known and not-so-well-known cooks to give short presentations there. We also invited Christopher Hirsheimer and Melissa Hamilton to photograph the presenters. Christopher and Melissa's portraits of the cooks appear here with the simple techniques they demonstrated, which I have explained in my own voice, sometimes illustrating them with my own slightly different recipes, while remaining as faithful to their intentions as possible. (The demonstrations can also be seen online, at www.alicewatersgreenkitchen.com.) I've also included additional recipes of my own, and some elementary guidelines for equipping your own green kitchen and for stocking it with the provisions you need for fresh and healthy meals.

At home in their own kitchens, even the most renowned chefs do not consider themselves to be chefs; there, they are simply cooks, preparing the simple, uncomplicated food they like best. Preparing food like that does not have to be hard work. On the contrary, the whole process—thinking about food, deciding what you want to eat, shopping for ingredients, and, finally, cooking and eating—is the purest pleasure, and too much fun to be reserved exclusively for "foodies." Cooking creates a sense of well-being for yourself and the people you love and brings beauty and meaning to everyday life. And all it requires is common sense—the common sense to eat seasonally, to know where your food comes from, to support and buy from local farmers and producers who are good stewards of our natural resources, and to apply the same principles of conservation to your own home kitchen.

All the good cooks I know are sensualists who take great pleasure in the beauty, smell, taste, and feel of the ingredients. They cook with their hands. Touch conveys so much about freshness, ripeness, condition, and texture. Our hands are amazingly sensitive tools. The best way to judge the doneness of a steak on the grill or a piece of fish in the oven is to touch it: How tender or resistant it feels will tell you how rare or cooked it is. The best way to toss a bowl of delicate salad greens is with your fingers: You won't crush the tender leaves and you can feel when there is enough, but not too much, dressing. With practice, your hands will remember, and these skills will become natural and automatic.

The value of learning a foundation of basic techniques is that once these skills become instinctive, you can cook comfortably and confidently without recipes, inspired by the ingredients you have. This book has recipes, of course, but they are intended as examples of methods and techniques that apply to all cooking everywhere. Once you have mastered a few dishes by making them repeatedly—such as a dinner of roast chicken with oven-roasted potatoes and turnips, and a garden salad with garlic vinaigrette—you will be rewarded with satisfying meals and a great sense of accomplishment. There is enormous pleasure in cooking good food simply and in sharing the cooking and the eating with friends and family. I think it is the best antidote to our overstressed modern lives. And there is nothing better than putting a plate of delicious food on the table for the people you love.

A Green Kitchen Manifesto

Delicious, affordable, wholesome food
is the goal of the green kitchen.

An organic pantry is an essential resource.

Buy food that is organic, local, and seasonal.

Cooking and shopping for food brings
rhythm and meaning to our lives.

Simple cooking techniques can be learned by heart.

Daily cooking improves the economy of the kitchen.

Cooking equipment that is durable and minimal
simplifies the cooking.

A garden brings life and beauty to the table.

Composting nourishes the land that feeds us.

Setting the table and eating together
teaches essential values to our children.

« STOCKING AN ORGANIC PANTRY »

The most important part of cooking is shopping and provisioning, before the real cooking begins. Not only is it difficult to make something delicious from inferior ingredients, but when you have raw food that has life and flavor, simple cooking is all that is needed. My mantra is: organic, local, and seasonal. Freshness is key. Vegetables and fruit just harvested have a vitality that you can see and taste and smell. That is one of the arguments for buying locally produced food; the closer you are to the source, the fresher the food is likely to be. That the food is organic is also critical. It will taste the best because it will have been grown in healthy soil. The food we eat is simply not wholesome if it contains harmful chemical residues. And by choosing to buy food from farmers and ranchers who produce food organically, we support the people who are taking care of the environment and nurturing the soil.

There are certain ingredients that I always want to have on hand in the kitchen. They fall into two general categories: the less perishable stores like oils and vinegars, and rice and beans, which are replenished less frequently; and the very perishable fresh produce, dairy, eggs, and meats, which are in constant rotation through the kitchen.

Olive oils and vinegars	Fresh herbs and salad greens
Salts and peppercorns	Garlic and shallots
Chile peppers and spices	Onions, carrots, and celery
Pastas and noodles	Seasonal vegetables and fruit
Rice and dried beans	Meat, poultry, and fish
Teas, coffee, and wine	Milk and eggs
Flours and sugar	Butter and cheese
Baking powder and soda	Chicken stock
Vanilla and vanilla beans	Nuts and bread

Regular shopping routines are pleasing, efficient, and economical—both the once- or twice-a-week trips to the farmers' market for staples and the once-a-year trips for such inspiring seasonal arrivals as the first cherries and apricots, or the first fresh shelling beans and striped eggplants. Having a select and thoughtfully stocked pantry, knowing you always have a few good things at home to cook and eat, means you have something to look forward to and cooking can be a joy, not a chore.

Olive Oils & Vinegars

There is a dizzying array of olive oils to choose from and dizzying prices to match, so it is helpful to understand the terms on the label. There are two categories of olive oil defined by how they are processed: virgin oil and refined oil. Virgin oil is pressed and filtered without heat or chemical processing. "Extra-virgin" oil is the highest grade; it has the best flavor and lowest acidity level. "Virgin" oil is produced by the same method, but it has a milder flavor and it can have a higher acidity level. Refined oils have undergone a chemical process to neutralize strong flavors or defects in the oil. Pure olive oil is usually a neutral-tasting blend of virgin and refined oil. Virgin oils do not contain any refined oil.

Most olive oil on the market comes from Mediterranean countries; a smaller amount is produced in California and other parts of the globe. Olive oils are comparable to grapes and wine in that many factors determine their quality and taste: olive variety, climate, soil, ripeness at harvest time, and age. Some extra-virgin oils have soft, buttery qualities, others have grassy and herbaceous flavors, some are hot and spicy tasting, and most have a lingering peppery finish.

Extra-virgin oils are the most intensely flavored and are best used uncooked, for salads, sauces, and finishing additions to soups and vegetables, because their flavors can be compromised by heating. A lesser quality (and less expensive) extra-virgin or virgin oil is better for sautéing and all-purpose use. I recommend having a few different oils on hand for different uses, depending on your budget and how much oil you use. Olive oil is perishable. It is at its peak when freshly pressed, but its aromas and flavors gradually diminish over time and it is best consumed within a year of harvest. Once opened, use it up within a few months and, if possible, store it in a cool place out of the sun.

High price doesn't guarantee quality. There are many extremely expensive fancy bottles of oil from boutique producers that don't seem to justify the cost. Specialty food stores and high-end supermarkets are probably the best places to shop for oil. Some offer samples for tasting and sell oils in bulk, and allow choices in a range of quantities. Finding oil that suits your taste at an economical price is a matter of trial and error. Ask your friends what they're cooking with; the same goes for vinegars. I like to ask at restaurants as well; if I taste a particularly good vinaigrette on a salad, I'll ask what oil and vinegar they're using in the kitchen.

Walnut and hazelnut oils are intensely nutty in flavor and very good in salad dressings with bitter greens and chicories, and with fall fruits such as pears, persimmons, apples, and figs. Nut oils can taste very strong on their own and are better used in combination with mild olive oil. They are also quite perishable and can become rancid in a short time once opened. Store them in the refrigerator and use them up within a month or two.

Neutral-tasting peanut oil or vegetable oil is a good choice for deep-frying or frying at hot temperatures. Most have a smoke point well above the average frying temperature of 375°F. Olive oil has a lower smoke point and is not the best choice for high-temperature frying.

I keep several different kinds of vinegars on hand: red wine vinegar, champagne and white wine vinegars, sherry vinegar, and balsamic vinegar. As with olive oils and other ingredients, quality varies. Inexpensive wine vinegars are often made from bad wine and taste like it. Good-quality unpasteurized wine vinegar is the best. The most flavorful ones will cost more, but they are worth it. Considering that you typically use vinegar in very small amounts, that added flavor goes a long way. Genuine balsamic vinegar is aged, highly concentrated, and very expensive; it is meant to be used sparingly drop by drop. Most commercial balsamic vinegars are considerably less expensive and quite sweet. I find they are most useful when blended with other flavorful wine vinegars to balance the sweetness. Other combinations of vinegars are interesting, too—sherry vinegar with white or red wine vinegar is good for dressing many vegetable and fruit salads. Experiment to find what you like. Cider vinegar is good for pickling vegetables, and rice wine vinegar is good for flavoring sushi rice and for dressing Asian-style salads and pickles.

For those who have the interest and wherewithal, you can make excellent vinegar at home. It's a great way to use the remains of the occasional unfinished bottle of wine. You will need a large glass jug covered at the top with a double thickness of cheesecloth (the vinegar needs to breathe), or a small wooden vinegar cask with a bunghole at the top for adding wine and a small spigot at the bottom to draw off the vinegar. You can find what you need at a store that sells winemaking supplies. The cask or glass container should be inoculated with an unpasteurized vinegar, which will contain what is called a vinegar mother, the cloudy and harmless mass you sometimes find suspended in a bottle of vinegar. This "mother" is the bacterial culture that converts the alcohol in wine to acetic acid, turning it to vinegar. The better the quality of the wine added to the vinegar barrel, the better tasting the resulting vinegar will be.

« GREEN KITCHEN TECHNIQUES »

FANNY SINGER is my daughter and fellow salad lover. When she was very young, I could get her to try almost anything if I gave her a little bowl of vinaigrette for dipping. Now she delights in finding all kinds of salad treasures at the farmers' market, such as these beautiful chicories, and she not only loves cooking, she loves writing about food.

« WASHING LETTUCE »

I could eat a salad at every meal, including breakfast with a poached egg and toast. Most of the time, I serve salad alongside other dishes, and not as a separate course before or after. A salad of fresh greens with a tart vinaigrette refreshes the palate and is a bright counterpart to almost anything else, and especially to rich or fatty foods. A real salad makes a far tastier garnish on the plate than an undressed sprig of parsley or watercress—it's not just decor, it's for eating.

To wash lettuce, fill a large basin with cold water—your kitchen sink or a large bowl. Before washing heads of lettuce, remove any damaged outer leaves and cut off the stem ends. Separate the leaves, dropping them into the water, and swish them around with your hands. Leave the lettuce in the water a minute or two to let any dirt or sand settle to the bottom, then lift the leaves out of the water and into a colander to drain. If the lettuce is still gritty, change the water and wash again.

Dry the lettuce thoroughly. If the leaves are wet, the dressing won't stick and its flavor will be diluted. Put the leaves into a salad spinner in small batches, no more than half full at a time, and spin the leaves dry. Empty the water from the spinner after each batch. Lay the leaves out in a single layer on a clean dish towel and roll the towel up. (If you don't have a salad spinner, drain the lettuce in a colander before layering the leaves between towels and rolling the towels up.) Refrigerate until you are ready to dress and serve the salad.

« DRESSING A SALAD »

Garlic vinaigrette is the dressing I make most often. The quantities that follow are only an approximate guide because garlics, vinegars, and oils vary so much in strength and intensity. The first step in making a vinaigrette is to macerate garlic in vinegar and salt. The vinegar softens the raw taste of the garlic, and the salt tames the sharp edge of the vinegar. Sometimes I like to mix different kinds of vinegar; a few drops of balsamic vinegar can temper a wine vinegar that's too strong. Taste for balance and adjust by adding more salt or vinegar; it should be neither too salty nor too acidic. The mixture should taste delicious by itself.

GARLIC VINAIGRETTE
4 SERVINGS

1 small garlic clove
Salt
2 tablespoons red wine vinegar

Fresh-ground black pepper
3 to 4 tablespoons olive oil

Put a peeled garlic clove and 2 big pinches of salt in a mortar and pound into a purée, with no chunks remaining. Add the wine vinegar, grind in some black pepper, and taste for the balance of salt and vinegar. Allow to macerate for a few minutes, and whisk in olive oil. Taste the dressing with a leaf of lettuce. It should taste bright and lively without being too acidic or too oily; adjust the salt, vinegar, or oil as needed.

To dress a salad, put several generous handfuls of washed and dried lettuce in a large bowl. Toss with about three quarters of the vinaigrette, and taste. The lettuce should be lightly coated but not overdressed; add more dressing as needed.

» Use a finely diced shallot instead of, or in addition to, the garlic paste.
» A squeeze of lemon juice added to the dressed salad at the last moment can add a brightness that brings up all the flavors.

HEARTS OF ROMAINE & GREEN GODDESS DRESSING
4 TO 6 SERVINGS

This is a tangy, creamy, and herbaceous version of a classic dressing that is well paired with crisp and sturdy romaine lettuce. Use whole uncut leaves; if the heads are large, you may need to remove many of the outer leaves to get to the pale green sweet leaves at the heart. Little Gem and Winter Density are small tender varieties that are perfect for this dressing and for Caesar salad.

2 or 3 heads romaine lettuce,
    or 6 to 8 heads Little Gem
1 shallot
1 garlic clove
3 tablespoons white wine vinegar
3 tablespoons lemon juice
2 salt-packed whole anchovies
½ ripe avocado
¾ cup olive oil

½ cup whipping cream
¼ cup chopped Italian parsley
3 tablespoons chopped tarragon
2 tablespoons chopped cilantro
1 tablespoon chopped basil
Fresh-ground black pepper
Salt
3 tablespoons chopped chives

Remove the outer dark leaves from the romaine lettuce, or any damaged outer leaves from the Little Gems. Cut off the stem ends and separate the leaves. Wash the leaves thoroughly and spin-dry in batches. Roll them up in a clean dish towel and refrigerate until ready to serve.

Peel and finely dice the shallot and garlic, and in a medium bowl, macerate in the white wine vinegar and lemon juice. Rinse, bone, and finely chop the anchovies and add to the bowl. Add the avocado flesh and mash the mixture with a fork. Whisking with the fork, gradually incorporate the olive oil and cream, as if making a thin mayonnaise. Stir in the parsley, tarragon, cilantro, and basil, and add a few grinds of black pepper and a pinch of salt. Taste and add more salt or vinegar if needed.

Arrange the lettuce in a large bowl, on a platter, or on individual plates, and pour the dressing over the leaves. Sprinkle with the chives and serve.

Cherry Tomato & Tofu Salad

2 SERVINGS

This is a salad that David Chang (page 80) made in the Green Kitchen. David's cooking often applies traditional Asian flavorings and methods to the foods of this continent. This salad is similar to a tomato and mozzarella salad, but it is quite different and surprising in its combination of flavors.

2 teaspoons soy sauce

A few drops of toasted sesame oil

A dash of sherry vinegar

1 to 2 tablespoons olive oil

Sea salt

Fresh-ground black pepper

1 teaspoon sesame seeds

1 cup ripe cherry tomatoes, halved

2 slices very fresh tofu or yuba (tofu skin), ½ inch thick and about 2 by 4 inches

Shiso leaves

Combine the soy sauce, sesame oil, vinegar, and olive oil, and season with salt and pepper to taste. Toasted sesame oil is very potent and should be used sparingly. Add the dressing and the sesame seeds to the cherry tomatoes and mix together. Arrange the tofu on a plate and spoon over the tomatoes and dressing. Cut fresh shiso leaves into fine ribbons, or tear the leaves into pieces, and scatter over the tomatoes and tofu, then serve.

TRACI DES JARDINS is an impassioned chef with three fine San Francisco restaurants—Jardinière, the Acme Chophouse, and Mijita. She grew up on a farm in the San Joaquin Valley, and she's never lost her empathy for everyone up and down the food chain, from farmer to diner. She is one of the champions of the Bay Area food community.

« FLAVORING A SAUCE »

A simple uncooked sauce of fresh herbs brings aliveness to the table. Salsa verde (green sauce) is a versatile sauce of parsley and olive oil flavored with shallots, capers, and lemon zest. The basic recipe can be enhanced with additional ingredients to make it more pungent and complex. It will brighten and complement many dishes, especially grilled vegetables, meat, and fish.

SALSA VERDE
MAKES ABOUT ¾ CUP

1 garlic clove, peeled
1 tablespoon capers, rinsed
2 salt-packed anchovy fillets,
    rinsed (optional)
1 shallot, peeled and finely diced
Grated zest of 1 lemon

½ cup Italian parsley leaves,
    washed, dried, and chopped
About ½ cup olive oil
Salt and fresh-ground black pepper

In a mortar, pound the garlic and capers (and anchovies, if you like) to a paste. (Or, if you don't have a mortar, chop them together very fine.) Stir in the shallot, lemon zest, freshly chopped parsley, and olive oil, and season with salt and pepper to taste. Let the salsa sit for 30 minutes or so for the flavors to develop, then taste again for seasoning. Add more or less oil depending on what you're serving it with; grilled meat and vegetables might want less oil, fish a bit more.

» Variations to salsa verde:
Add other fresh tender-leaved herbs to the parsley, such as chervil, chives, cilantro, tarragon, basil, or mint.
Use diced red onion in place of the shallot and eliminate the garlic.
Add finely chopped fresh chile pepper to spice it up.
Add chopped hard-cooked egg and a little Dijon-style mustard.
Add lightly toasted and chopped almonds, walnuts, or pine nuts.
Add lemon juice or vinegar, but just before serving so the acid doesn't discolor the herbs.
» A similar sauce without oil, called gremolata, is made of chopped garlic, parsley, and lemon zest; it makes a bright garnish for grilled foods, braised meats, or pasta.

Left to right, top row: peppermint; spearmint; thyme; parsley; basil; cilantro; bay laurel.
Left to right, bottom row: marjoram; tarragon; chervil; chives; savory; rosemary; sage; lemon verbena.

JOAN NATHAN is the preeminent chronicler and curator of Jewish-American culinary tradition. I once had the privilege of going to Russia with Joan Nathan, and everywhere we went, she taught me to see beneath the surface to the deep culture below. Her cookbooks go beneath the surface, too.

« POUNDING A SAUCE »

A mortar and pestle is an ancient tool unimproved by modern technology. Pounding ingredients in a mortar is very sensual. I think it helps you understand how to balance the flavors of a sauce; as you pound and blend the various elements, you can smell and taste their qualities and intensity. A mortar allows you to control the texture of an ingredient or a mixture without overworking. The uneven texture of basil leaves, nuts, and cheese in a pesto sauce pounded by hand is more interesting than the uniform and airy mixture produced by a machine. The chunky texture of a guacamole or tomato salsa made in a mortar makes the flavors seem more distinct and complex. Plus, pounding is more fun than flipping a switch.

PESTO SAUCE
MAKES ABOUT 1½ CUPS

Pesto is a traditional pasta sauce, but it is also a delicious sauce for grilled vegetables and chicken, salads, and pizzas, and a perfect final flavoring to a bean and vegetable soup.

1 or 2 small garlic cloves
Salt
¼ cup pine nuts or walnuts,
   lightly toasted

1 bunch basil (1 cup leaves)
¼ cup grated Parmesan cheese
About ½ cup olive oil

Peel and slice the garlic and put it in a large mortar. (You may want to take out some of the garlic and add it later if more is needed after tasting. The garlic flavor should not overwhelm the perfume of the basil.) Add a pinch of salt and the nuts, and pound the mixture to a paste. Add the basil leaves, and continue pounding and grinding the leaves until they are somewhat smooth. Work in the cheese and the oil. Add more or less oil depending on the thickness desired. Taste and add more salt if needed.

» Italian parsley or rocket can be substituted for the basil, with or without the cheese.

GILBERT PILGRAM, now a restaurateur in his own right (at Zuni Café in San Francisco, with Judy Rodgers), was once an untrained but highly motivated volunteer in the Chez Panisse kitchens—so highly motivated, and so in tune with our philosophy, that he soon became an accomplished chef and, ultimately, our general manager. Like his personality, his palate is unconventional and wide awake.

GUACAMOLE

MAKES ABOUT 2 CUPS

The simplest guacamole is made with avocado, onions, jalapeño, lime, salt, and cilantro. The amounts of the ingredients can vary; guacamole is very forgiving. The important things are to taste for a balance of salt, heat, and acid and to make the guacamole taste the way you like it.

2 large ripe avocados	2 or 3 small juicy limes
Salt	1 jalapeño pepper
4 green onions	Cilantro

Halve the avocados, remove the pits, scoop out the flesh into a mortar, and season with salt. Trim and slice the green onions, and put them in a small bowl, add salt, and squeeze in the juice of 2 limes—macerating the onions in lime juice softens their raw taste. Cut off the stem end of the jalapeño, cut the pepper in half lengthwise, and remove the membranes and seeds. Flatten the pepper and cut into fine dice. Mash the avocado, but leave it a bit chunky. Add the onions and lime juice, along with the jalapeño, either all or part, depending on how spicy you like your guacamole, and mix lightly. Taste and add more salt and lime juice as needed. Chop a handful of fresh cilantro stems and leaves, and stir into the guacamole. Serve with tortilla chips.

» If you like, add a diced ripe tomato to the guacamole. Gilbert's advice: Don't bother to peel it; Mexican cooks never do.

RICK BAYLESS, many years ago, made me the first tacos I really fell in love with—they were simple, wonderfully porky tacos, with beautiful, uncomplicated salsas. He is a brilliant teacher with an inexhaustible curiosity about authentic Mexican cooking. His Chicago restaurants owe their excellence in part to his commitment to his staff: When he travels for research and inspiration, he takes them along.

ROASTED TOMATO OR TOMATILLO SALSA
MAKES ABOUT 2 CUPS

In Mexico, salsas are typically made with ingredients roasted on a clay *comal*, or griddle. A cast-iron skillet is a good substitute. When whole chile peppers, unpeeled garlic cloves, tomatoes, and tomatillos are dry-roasted, they brown as they cook and develop the toasty overtones that create deep flavors in the salsa. Another traditional tool is the *molcajete y tejolote*, a rough stone mortar and pestle used to mash and blend the salsa.

2 serrano chiles

2 large garlic cloves

4 medium-size ripe tomatoes, or 4 large tomatillos

1 small onion

Salt

1 lime

Handful of cilantro leaves, chopped

Heat a skillet over medium-high heat. Put the whole chiles and the garlic cloves, unpeeled in the pan. Core the tomatoes and cut them in half. If cooking tomatillos, remove the husks and cut the tomatillos in half. Add the tomatoes or tomatillos to the pan, and cook the vegetables for 10 minutes or so, until they start to soften and brown. Turn them over to brown on the other side, and cook until tender throughout, then remove from the pan.

Squeeze the soft garlic cloves out of the skins. Remove the stems from the serranos and slice the chiles. Combine the garlic and chiles in the mortar and grind to a paste. Add the tomatoes, with or without the skins, and mash them to blend thoroughly with the garlic and chiles. Peel and finely dice the onion, put it in a small strainer, and rinse in water to crisp the onion and take away some of the raw bite. Stir the onion into the salsa and season with salt, a squeeze of lime juice, and the chopped cilantro.

» Green tomatillo salsa is very good with diced fresh avocado added at the end; you may need to add a little water to thin the salsa.

JÉRÔME WAAG is a San Francisco performance artist who is also a Chez Panisse chef. His food and his art share the same imagination, discipline, and wit. The son of an old friend in Provence, he's been cooking with me since he was twelve years old, when he was already making art and training his eye to see things his way. Today his cooking is never conventional, but it always shows reverence for the ingredients.

« WHISKING MAYONNAISE »

Homemade mayonnaise is so superior to store-bought that it is well worth the effort. Some people are intimidated by the thought of making a mayonnaise, but it is a skill easily mastered. A mayonnaise made with garlic, or aïoli, is one of my favorite sauces for almost everything.

In the fall and winter months, garlic cloves may have a green sprouting germ in the center. Cut each clove in half lengthwise before pounding, and remove the bitter germ.

GARLIC MAYONNAISE
MAKES ABOUT 1 CUP

2 or 3 garlic cloves
Salt
1 egg yolk

About ½ teaspoon water
1 cup olive oil

Peel and slice the garlic. Put it in a mortar along with a pinch of salt, and pound into a smooth paste.

In a medium bowl, whisk together about half the garlic, the egg yolk, and about ½ teaspoon water (adding a bit of water to the egg yolk at the outset helps to stabilize the mixture). Slowly dribble the oil into the egg mixture, whisking constantly. As the egg yolk absorbs the oil, the mixture will thicken and lighten in color. When it reaches that point, you can add the oil a little faster, still whisking continuously. If the mixture becomes very thick before all the oil is incorporated, thin with a few drops of water. Taste and add more salt and garlic, as desired. If not serving the mayonnaise right away, refrigerate it. Garlic mayonnaise will taste better after about half an hour, and it should be eaten the same day it is made.

» Plain mayonnaise is made this way, but without the garlic, and finished with a few drops of lemon juice or vinegar. It can be flavored in many ways: with the addition of fresh herbs such as parsley, basil, watercress, chervil, tarragon, or chives, chopped or pounded in a mortar; mustard; anchovies, boned and pounded or finely chopped; capers or pickles, rinsed and chopped; or finely chopped chile pepper.

Grand Aïoli

4 to 6 servings

In the south of France, an aïoli is both the garlic and olive oil mayonnaise sauce itself and the dish for which it is the raison d'être, which can be either *grand* or *petit*. *Le grand aïoli* is a festive Provençal free-for-all meal in itself, typically consisting of the sauce in its mortar surrounded by platters of seasonal vegetables (cauliflower, carrots, beets, green beans, artichokes, potatoes) all freshly boiled; poached salt cod and stewed octopus; and tomatoes and hard-boiled eggs.

Summer is the time for an aïoli extravaganza; with crisp cold rosé wine, it is the perfect dish on a hot evening. Garlic is juicy and firm and in season, and the summer vegetables that are so good with the garlic mayonnaise are plentiful. The ingredients listed below are suggestions; add whatever vegetables and fish you like.

2 cups Garlic Mayonnaise (page 27)
1 bunch baby carrots
1 small head cauliflower
8 ounces green beans
8 to 12 fingerling potatoes
Salt
2 red bell peppers
4 hard-cooked eggs

1 pound cherry tomatoes or other tomatoes
1 pound small squid, cod, halibut, or other fish
Fresh-ground pepper
Olive oil
Crusty bread

Make a double recipe of the Garlic Mayonnaise on the previous page. Use more garlic if you like an intense and pungent aïoli.

Trim and prepare the vegetables: Peel the carrots and leave them whole with half an inch or so of stems attached. Separate the cauliflower into florets of similar size. Top and tail the beans. If the potatoes are small, wash and leave them whole; otherwise, peel and cut into chunks of similar size. Bring a pot of salted water to a boil, and cook the prepared vegetables separately, until just tender. Roast the peppers, peel and seed them, and cut into strips (page 85). Or leave the peppers raw, cut out the membranes and seeds, and cut into strips. Peel the eggs, and cut into halves or quarters. Stem the cherry tomatoes and cut in half, or core larger tomatoes and cut into slices.

Clean the squid, season with salt and pepper, and thread the bodies and tentacles separately onto bamboo skewers. Grill the squid over a hot fire. If cooking fish, season the fish with salt and pepper, moisten with olive oil, and either grill or bake the fish until just cooked.

Arrange the vegetables, squid, and eggs on a large platter, and serve family-style with the aïoli and fresh crusty bread.

DARINA ALLEN founded the Ballymaloe Cookery School more than twenty-five years ago, on an organic farm in County Cork. A tireless and inspiring teacher, she is renowned for her food activism in Ireland and beyond. She understands how good cooking flourishes when children are introduced early to the kitchen and the garden, where they learn to eat wisely and well.

« MAKING BREAD »

Making your own bread is immensely satisfying. At the Green Kitchen, we had demonstrations of two very quick ways to put bread on your table: Darina's traditional Irish soda bread and Scott Peacock's buttermilk biscuits (page 33). Neither of these recipes requires the dough to sit for hours while it rises, because neither of them relies on yeast. Instead they are lightened by the chemical reaction that occurs between the buttermilk and the baking soda (or baking powder) when the dough goes into the oven. For this book, I've added a third recipe, this one for Jim Lahey's yeast bread (page 35). Jim, proprietor of the Sullivan Street Bakery in New York, has a brilliant method of making a country loaf that develops flavor in a long, slow rise, but which, like Darina's soda bread, requires no kneading at all. None of these three recipes is complicated.

Darina's soda bread is something I make at home all the time. From start to finish, you can have fresh bread in less than an hour.

IRISH SODA BREAD
MAKES 1 LARGE LOAF

4 cups unbleached all-purpose flour,   1 teaspoon salt
    or 2 cups unbleached all-purpose   1 teaspoon baking soda
    and 2 cups whole-wheat flour   1½ to 1¾ cups buttermilk

Preheat the oven to 450°F. Measure the flour, salt, and baking soda and put them through a sieve into a comfortably large bowl. Run your fingers through the flour to lift and aerate it. Make a well in the center and pour in 1½ cups buttermilk. To mix the buttermilk into the flour, use the fingers of one hand, stiff and outstretched, and stir in a big circle, working from the center out. The dough should be soft, but not sticky; add a bit more buttermilk if needed. In a few turns, you will have a moist shaggy dough.

Rinse your hands, and turn the dough out onto a floured board. Gently roll and pat it into a tidy round shape about 2 inches high. Don't knead the dough; it will make it tough. Put the ball of dough on a baking sheet. Cut a deep cross in the loaf from side to side, and poke a hole in each quarter. Bake for 15 minutes, reduce the heat to 400°F, and continue baking for another 25 to 30 minutes, until crusty and browned. The bread should sound hollow when tapped on the bottom. Let cool on a wire rack.

SCOTT PEACOCK is a champion of Southern cooking, both at Watershed, his restaurant in Decatur, Georgia, and in print, as co-author of *The Gift of Southern Cooking,* with the legendary Edna Lewis. In fact, though, his cooking would flourish anywhere: He cooks with the best ingredients and breathes new life into historical traditions.

BUTTERMILK BISCUITS
MAKES ABOUT FIFTEEN 2½-INCH BISCUITS

According to Scott, a biscuit should be crusty and golden brown on the top, with an interior that is soft, light, and tender. Purist that he is, he makes them with freshly rendered lard and recommends making your own fresh baking powder: Measure and sift together 3 times, 2 parts cream of tartar and 1 part baking soda. Make it in small batches, store in an airtight container, and use within 4 weeks.

A sweetened version of the biscuit dough (see page 34) makes delicious short-cakes to serve with whipped cream and sliced ripe fruit or berries and is great for making cobbler (page 127).

5 cups unbleached all-purpose flour
1 tablespoon plus 1½ teaspoons
    homemade baking powder
1 tablespoon kosher salt

½ cup plus 2 tablespoons cold
    good-quality lard or unsalted butter
1¾ to 2 cups buttermilk
3 tablespoons unsalted butter, melted

Preheat the oven to 500°F. Put the flour, baking powder, and salt in a large bowl, and blend thoroughly. Add the lard or butter (cut into pieces), and working quickly, lightly rub the lard and flour together with your fingertips until about half the lard is coarsely blended and the other half remains in large pieces about ½ inch in diameter.

Make a well in the flour mixture and pour in 1¾ cups buttermilk. Stir briefly, just until the dough is blended and begins to form a mass. The dough should be soft and a bit sticky and there should not be large amounts of unincorporated flour in the bowl. If the dough is too dry, add a few tablespoons more buttermilk.

Turn the dough onto a generously floured surface, and with floured hands, knead briskly 8 to 10 times until a cohesive dough is formed. Gently flatten the dough to an even thickness, and using a floured rolling pin, roll it out to a uniform thickness of ½ inch. With a floured dinner fork, pierce the dough completely through at ½-inch intervals.

Lightly flour a 2½- or 3-inch biscuit cutter and stamp out rounds. Avoid twisting the cutter as you stamp, and cut the biscuits as close together as possible for maximum yield. Arrange the biscuits on an ungreased or parchment-lined heavy baking sheet so that they almost touch. Don't reroll the scraps, just bake them as is and enjoy as a treat.

(continued)

Bake in the upper third of the oven for 8 to 12 minutes, until a crusty golden brown. If necessary, rotate the pan during the baking for even cooking. Remove from the oven, brush with the melted butter, and serve hot.

» To make Sweet Cream Biscuits for shortcake or cobbler (page 127): Add 3 tablespoons granulated sugar to the dry ingredients, and use butter instead of lard. Substitute 1 cup whipping cream and 1 cup half-and-half for the buttermilk. Bake the shortcake biscuits at 450°F for 10 to 15 minutes; to check if they are fully cooked, test one of the biscuits from the center of the sheet by gently pulling it apart.

No-Knead Bread

A crusty yeast-raised bread requires time and planning, but not necessarily more work, as Jim Lahey's recipe proves. Long, slow rising (fermentation) is the secret to this flavorful loaf of country-style bread.

3 cups unbleached bread flour
¼ teaspoon active dry yeast
1¼ teaspoons salt
1⅓ cups water
Olive oil

Extra flour, wheat bran, or cornmeal, for dusting
One 4½- to 5½-quart ovenproof heavy pot with a lid (Pyrex glass, cast iron, or earthenware)

Mix all of the dry ingredients in a medium bowl. Add the water, and mix by hand or with a wooden spoon for 30 seconds to 1 minute, until you have a wet, sticky dough. If it is not very sticky to the touch, mix in 1 or 2 more tablespoons of water. Cover the bowl with a plate or plastic wrap and let the dough rise for 12 to 18 hours at room temperature (approximately 72°F), until the surface is dotted with bubbles and the dough has more than doubled in size.

When the first rise is complete, generously dust a work surface with flour. Use a bowl scraper or rubber spatula to scrape the dough onto the surface in one piece. As the dough pulls away from the bowl, it will cling in long, thin strands (this is the developed gluten), and it will be quite loose and sticky; do not add more flour. Use lightly floured hands, a bowl scraper, or a spatula to lift the edges of the dough in toward the center. Tuck in the edges of the dough to make it round.

Generously coat a clean smooth cotton dish towel with flour, wheat bran, or cornmeal. Gently lift the dough and place it seam side down onto the towel, and lightly dust the dough with flour. Fold the ends of the towel loosely over the dough to cover it, and place it in a warm, draft-free spot to rise for 1 to 2 hours. The dough is ready when it is almost doubled, and when you gently poke it with your finger, it holds the impression. If it doesn't, let rise for another 15 minutes.

Thirty minutes before the end of the second rise, preheat the oven to 475°F. Position a rack in the lower third of the oven, and place the covered pot in the center of the rack. Carefully remove the preheated pot from the oven and un-cover it. Unfold the dish towel, lightly dust the dough with flour, and quickly but gently invert it into the pot, seam side up. Use caution, the pot will be very hot. Cover the pot and bake for 30 minutes.

Remove the lid, and continue baking for 15 to 30 minutes more, until the bread is a deep chestnut color. Use a spatula or pot holders to carefully lift the bread out of the pot, and place it on a rack to cool thoroughly, for 1 hour or more.

CLODAGH McKENNA trained and worked at Ballymaloe Cookery School for three years. She left the school to organize farmers' markets around Ireland. Today she is a food journalist, a cookbook author, and a television food star in the British Isles and New Zealand. I love watching Clodagh McKenna cook; she's young and dedicated, and her enthusiasm for slow food is infectious.

« TOASTING BREAD »

Croutons of various kinds are an essential part of the kitchen repertoire: as appetizers with tasty bites of fava bean purée or olive paste, or with butter and radishes or ripe tomatoes; or eaten with soup in the form of slices of crusty country-style bread brushed with olive oil and rubbed with garlic; or added to salads as bite-size croutons.

To make croutons, choose tasty, good-quality bread, either fresh or day-old. Slice the bread thinly or thickly, depending on your intended use. There are several ways to toast the slices. Brush with olive oil or melted butter, lay them out on a baking sheet, and toast in a 350°F oven until just golden brown at the edges. Keep an eye on them so they don't overcook. Or bake the slices until dry and then brush or drizzle with fruity olive oil while still warm from the oven. If you need only a few, toast the slices in a toaster or toaster oven and drizzle with oil when they're done. To make garlic croutons, lightly rub the croutons, while still warm from the oven, with a peeled raw garlic clove.

If you have a fire going and you're cooking on the grill, moisten the fresh slices of bread with olive oil, and toast over the coals on both sides, until lightly charred and crisp. Pay close attention; they are easily burned. Rub the croutons with a garlic clove while still warm. These are especially good to serve with anything juicy—salads, roasted meats or chicken and their pan juices, garlic mayonnaise—to soak up the tasty sauce or juices on the plate.

Torn croutons are good with mixed-lettuce and Caesar salads, and with juicy tomato salads. Cut off the crusts of a loaf of country-style bread, and tear the loaf into bite-size pieces. Pound 1 or 2 garlic cloves to a paste in a mortar and mix the garlic with olive oil. Put the torn pieces of bread in a bowl, add the garlic oil, and toss well. Spread out the croutons on a baking sheet and toast until just crisp.

Small, bite-size croutons fried in butter or oil add crunchy texture to salads and soups—they are especially good in puréed soups. Cut fine-textured bread into small cubes and fry them over medium heat in butter or olive oil. Add more butter or oil to the pan as it is absorbed by the croutons, if needed. They cook quickly, so keep a close eye on them, stirring or tossing frequently until they are crispy and golden brown. If you like, in the last moments of cooking, add chopped garlic and herbs to the pan with the croutons. Take care that the garlic does not brown.

Various breads for making croutons: baguette; white Pullman loaf; country-style levain loaf; multi-grain bread. Crouton toppings: salt-packed anchovy fillets; fava bean purée; tomatoes; olive paste; cheese and herbs.

BREADCRUMBS

Homemade breadcrumbs, freshly toasted and tossed with chopped herbs or fried herbs, are one of my favorite things. I use them as a crunchy finishing touch in many dishes, such as whole-wheat pasta with cherry tomatoes tossed in oil and vinegar, or pasta with spicy fried squid; and I use them to garnish grilled squash and eggplant, or to scatter over slices of roasted meat. Untoasted fresh breadcrumbs are good in stuffings and meatballs, for coating a chicken breast or a fish fillet to be fried, and for making a golden crust for vegetables that are roasted or gratinéed.

Breadcrumbs are best made from good-quality tasty bread that is a day or two old. For crumbs to be used for breading or frying, use fine-textured white bread such as a Pullman loaf or *pain-de-mie* (avoid bagged, sliced sandwich breads; the texture is too gummy for breadcrumbs). For toasted breadcrumbs, use white bread or coarse-textured levain or country-style bread.

Remove the crusts and cut the bread into cubes. Process the cubes in a blender or food processor in small batches. Crumbs for breading and frying should be ground fine. Fine crumbs stick easily and form an even coat. Crumbs for toasting can be ground more coarse.

Breading a fillet of fish or chicken in crumbs for frying is a three-step process. First dip the fillet in seasoned flour and shake off the excess. Next dip the floured fillet in beaten egg, and finally roll and pat in fresh breadcrumbs. The flour makes the egg stick, and the egg makes the breadcrumbs stick.

To toast breadcrumbs, toss them with about 1 tablespoon olive oil for every cup of breadcrumbs. Spread the crumbs on a rimmed baking sheet in a thin layer, and bake at 350°F until golden brown, stirring the crumbs every few minutes for even coloring. If you like, toss them with finely chopped garlic and with freshly chopped herbs—parsley, thyme, rosemary, tarragon, marjoram, and oregano, singly or in combination. Or fry leaves of fresh sage, rosemary, parsley, savory, or oregano in olive oil for a minute or so, until crisp, and mix with the toasted crumbs.

ANGELO GARRO is a San Francisco blacksmith whose Renaissance Forge is also a soulful kitchen where Angelo's guests sample the flavors of his native Sicily—all made from local California ingredients that he hunts, fishes, or harvests himself. He cures olives and salamis; he makes his own wine and grappa; and he is constantly gathering all the fresh wild things the seasons have to offer.

« POACHING AN EGG »

Poaching is a way of gently cooking an egg by submerging it in barely simmering liquid. Fill a shallow heavy-bottomed pan with 2 to 3 inches of water and bring to a simmer. Lower the heat to just under boiling, so there are no bubbles breaking the surface. Salt the water and, if you like, add a splash of vinegar. Carefully crack a fresh egg into a small cup or bowl. (Angelo has a trick of putting the egg into the water for 10 seconds to set the white just a bit before he cracks the egg into the bowl.) Hold the bowl or cup right at the level of the water and slide the egg in. Depending on its size and temperature, the egg will take 3 to 5 minutes to cook to the point at which the white is opaque and just set but the yolk is still soft. To test for doneness, use a slotted spoon to lift the egg out of the water and gently press with your finger to feel if the white has set. When the egg is done, remove and drain for a moment on a clean dish towel before serving.

For breakfast, Angelo likes poached eggs with a tomato and herb bruschetta: Dice ripe tomatoes and macerate with a peeled clove of garlic cut in half and some chopped parsley and oregano; moisten with olive oil and a splash of vinegar; and season with salt and pepper. Toast slices of crusty bread, top with the tomatoes and their juices (remove the garlic pieces first), and set the warm eggs on top of the tomatoes. Finish the eggs with salt, a drizzle of red wine vinegar and olive oil, and chopped oregano.

» Eggs are delicious poached in soups: for example, in a chicken broth with sliced croutons; in a spicy Mexican chicken soup with lime, cilantro, and fried tortilla strips; or in a garlic broth with diced fresh tomatoes and Parmesan cheese.

BOILED EGGS

To cook eggs in the shell, soft-boiled or hard-cooked, fill a pot with water deep enough to cover eggs by an inch or two, and bring to a boil. Reduce the heat to a gentle simmer and lower the eggs into the pot with a slotted spoon. For soft-boiled eggs with a runny yolk, simmer for 5 to 6 minutes. (If the eggs are very large or very small, adjust the timing by a minute more or a minute less.) Remove the eggs, cool briefly in cold water, and serve in the shell with the top cut off, or cracked open and scooped into a warm bowl. For hard-cooked eggs, with yolks just set but still moist at the center, simmer the eggs for 9 minutes. (For eggs with firmer yolks, simmer another minute or two.) Remove and cool in cold water, then crack them all over and peel off the shells.

FRIED EGGS

A heavy pan, such as a cast-iron skillet, is good for frying eggs. The heat is very even, and if the pan is well-seasoned, the eggs won't stick. Fried eggs tend to stick in stainless steel pans. Warm the pan over medium heat for a minute or two, add a thin layer of olive oil (eggs are delicious cooked in olive oil) or a nut of butter, and crack open the eggs into the pan. Lower the heat, season the eggs with salt and pepper and, if you like, a generous amount of chopped herbs—parsley, sage, chives, chervil, marjoram, basil. Cook gently until the eggs are set on the bottom and a little lacey around the edges, then cover the pan and cook until the whites are just set and the yolks are soft and runny; if you like the yolk more firm, cook it a little longer. Serve immediately.

SCRAMBLED EGGS

Again, the trusty cast-iron skillet is my first choice for cooking scrambled eggs. A 10-inch pan works well for up to a dozen eggs. Crack 1 or 2 eggs per person into a bowl, season with salt and pepper and, if you like, chopped herbs such as marjoram, chives, chervil, and parsley. Heat the pan over medium heat for a few minutes. When it is hot, add 1 or more tablespoons of butter. Beat the eggs lightly and when the butter is foaming, pour the eggs into the pan. Let the eggs cook until they begin to set, then stir them gently and slowly until they are cooked as loosely or firmly as you like. Take them off the heat a little before fully cooked; they will continue to cook in the time it takes to spoon them from the pan. Serve immediately.

BETH WELLS has been one of the two co-chefs at the Chez Panisse Café since 2008. She grew up in Texas, on the Gulf Coast, studied nutrition and cooking, and moved swiftly up the ranks in the Panisse kitchen. At home in Berkeley, Beth tends a large kitchen garden; every year she visits her partner's family in a village in the Spanish Pyrenees, and every year her admiration for Spanish cuisine grows stronger.

« SIMMERING A STOCK »

Not only is homemade stock easy to make and economical, but it also tastes better than any you can buy. I always like to have a quart of fresh stock on hand—or in the freezer—because then I know I have the makings of many a meal, notably a soup of seasonal vegetables. A whole chicken makes the most flavorful stock; otherwise, the meatier the chicken parts you use, the better. Sometimes I cut off the breasts of a chicken to save for another meal, and make stock with the rest of the bird. Whenever you roast a chicken, freeze the carcass to save for making stock; add it along with the other chicken parts.

CHICKEN STOCK
MAKES ABOUT 5 QUARTS

1 whole chicken, or meaty chicken parts (about 4 pounds)	1 head garlic, halved (optional)
1½ gallons cold water	1 whole leek, split in half and rinsed
1 carrot, peeled	1 teaspoon salt
1 onion, peeled and halved	A few black peppercorns
1 celery stalk	A few sprigs of parsley and thyme
	1 or 2 bay leaves

Put the chicken in a large pot and pour in 1½ gallons cold water. Over high heat, bring the water to a boil, and then turn the heat down low so that the broth is barely simmering, with bubbles just breaking the surface. Skim off the foam that rises to the top, but leave some of the fat; it adds lots of flavor to the stock and can be removed at the end. For a nice clear stock, do not let it boil again, or the fat and the liquid may emulsify, turning the stock cloudy and greasy. After skimming, add the vegetables, salt, peppercorns, and herbs and continue to simmer for 3 to 4 hours. (If you are in a hurry, you can use the stock after about an hour, before it is fully cooked.) Turn off the heat, let the stock cool a bit, and then strain.

Ladle the stock out of the pot and pass it through a fine strainer into a non-reactive container, or several small containers, for freezing. If using the stock right away, skim the fat. Otherwise, let the stock cool and refrigerate it with the fat, which will solidify on top and can then be easily removed. The stock will keep, covered, in the refrigerator for up to 1 week or for several months in the freezer.

CHICKEN NOODLE SOUP WITH DILL

4 SERVINGS

This is the soup I always make when I want something comforting and re-storative. This method easily becomes second-nature and is good for all kinds of seasonal vegetable soups: Soften the vegetables in oil or butter, add stock, and simmer until the vegetables are tender. Flavor with herbs, and, for a more substantial soup, add cooked pasta, beans, or, as in this recipe, chicken. Brothy vegetable soups are even better with a plate of garlic croutons (see page 37) to dip in the soup.

Olive oil
1 small onion, peeled and diced
1 carrot, peeled and diced
1 small celery stalk, diced
2 garlic cloves, peeled and chopped
1 leek, white part only, diced and
    rinsed (optional)

1 parsnip, peeled and diced (optional)
Salt
4 cups chicken stock (page 47)
1 chicken breast, skin removed
4 ounces dried fettuccine pasta
2 tablespoons chopped dill
A squeeze of lemon juice (optional)

Heat a heavy-bottomed saucepan over medium heat and add a few tablespoons of olive oil. Add the vegetables, season with salt, and cook gently for 10 to 15 minutes. Add the stock and bring to a simmer. Poach the chicken breast in the soup for 10 to 15 minutes, until just cooked through. Remove the chicken and let cool, then shred into bite-size pieces.

Break the fettuccine 2 or 3 times, into shorter lengths, and cook in a separate pot of boiling salted water until tender; drain and add to the soup just before serving, along with the chicken and dill. Taste; add more salt if needed and, if you like, a squeeze of lemon juice to brighten the flavors.

» For a lighter soup, omit the fettuccine and add 4 cups or so of baby spinach leaves and, if available, 1 cup of freshly shelled peas. Simmer for 5 to 8 minutes, until tender, and serve with freshly chopped parsley or chervil in place of the dill.

LENTIL SOUP
4 TO 6 SERVINGS

French green lentils are plump and speckled dark green. They are very flavorful, hold their shape when cooked, and are good for making salads and soups. For this rustic lentil soup, the lentils are cooked until they are tender and can be easily mashed—longer than they would be for a salad. The yogurt garnish brightens the earthy flavor of the rosemary and lentils.

3 to 4 tablespoons olive oil
2 carrots, peeled and diced
½ onion, peeled and diced
2 celery stalks, diced
2½ teaspoons kosher salt
3 garlic cloves, peeled and crushed

1 teaspoon chopped rosemary
1 cup French green lentils
7 cups water or chicken stock
  (page 47)
Fresh-ground black pepper
¼ cup plain yogurt

Heat a saucepan over medium-high heat and add 1 tablespoon of the olive oil to coat the bottom of the pan. Add the carrots, onion, celery, and 1 teaspoon salt and cook for about 5 minutes, until the vegetables begin to dry and soften. Reduce the heat to medium-low, and cook for 5 minutes more, stirring occasionally, until the carrots are tender and the onion is translucent. Add the garlic and rosemary to the saucepan and cook briefly to release their aroma.

Add the lentils and stir while adding the water and remaining 1½ teaspoons salt. Increase the heat to high, bring to a boil, then reduce the heat to low and simmer for 1 hour, stirring occasionally, until the lentils crush easily and have a creamy texture. Mash the lentils in the pan using a whisk or potato masher to thicken the soup, and season with pepper. Taste and add more salt if needed. Serve hot with a drizzle of yogurt and olive oil in each bowl.

» Serve the soup with hot and fluffy rice for a more substantial dish.
» For a spicier version, add chopped chiles to the vegetables at the beginning of the cooking. Or briefly sizzle cumin seeds in olive oil and stir into the soup before serving.

LEEK & POTATO SOUP
6 SERVINGS

This is a good soup to make in the fall months when mature leeks are at their flavorful peak and are plentiful in the markets. It is a traditional French soup that is typically puréed, but I prefer it with a clear chicken broth and sliced vegetables.

2 pounds leeks
3 tablespoons olive oil or butter
1 tablespoon chopped thyme
1 bay leaf
1 pound Yukon Gold or Yellow
  Finn potatoes
6 cups chicken stock (page 47)

Salt
Champagne or white wine vinegar
  (optional)
Fresh-ground black pepper
2 tablespoons chopped Italian
  parsley or chives

Prepare the leeks: Trim off the root ends and the tough upper green tops. Halve the white part of the leeks lengthwise and then, without cutting through the root end, cut lengthwise into ¼-inch-wide strips. Then cut the leeks crosswise into ¼-inch dice. Wash the diced leeks thoroughly in a large basin of cold water. Once the dirt has settled, scoop them out with a sieve or strainer. Drain and set aside.

Heat a heavy-bottomed pot over medium heat. Add the olive oil or butter, followed by the leeks, thyme, and bay leaf. Cook, stirring occasionally, until the leeks are tender, about 10 minutes. Peel the potatoes and cut them into ¼-inch dice or slices. Add the potatoes to the pot and cook for 3 to 4 minutes. Pour in the chicken stock, season with salt, and bring to a boil. Reduce the heat to maintain a low simmer, and continue cooking until the potatoes are tender, but not falling apart. Taste for salt and adjust as needed. Let the soup cool to room temperature, and refrigerate for several hours or overnight.

Before serving, remove the bay leaf and reheat the soup over medium heat and taste again for salt. If you like, add a splash of champagne or white wine vinegar to sharpen the flavors. Ladle the soup into warm serving bowls. Finish with a few grinds of the peppermill, and garnish with chopped parsley or chives.

» Vegetable soups often taste best several hours later or the following day. If time allows, make ahead and reheat gently before serving.
» Remove the bay leaf, and purée the soup before serving. Garnish with small fried croutons (see page 37) along with the herbs.
» Stir in ⅓ cup heavy cream before serving.

CHARLIE TROTTER of Chicago is one of our most famous chefs in America, and justifiably so. Although his restaurants and cookbooks epitomize an artistry and perfectionism that may seem out of reach to most home cooks, when Charlie demonstrates something routine that he does in his own home kitchen, he demystifies good cooking and makes it look completely attainable.

« PEELING TOMATOES »

All through the cold months, we wait for the real tomatoes of summer (bland out-of-season tomatoes don't count), until we find ourselves inundated with varieties of all kinds from late July until the fall. The pleasant challenge becomes how to use them all—in sauces, salads, gratins, sandwiches, soups, pastas. Peeling and seeding tomatoes is a summertime ritual.

Heat a pot of water to boiling and have ready a bowl of icy cold water. Drop the tomatoes, a few at a time, into the boiling water for 15 to 30 seconds, just long enough to loosen their skins. Very ripe tomatoes take less time, thick-skinned, firm tomatoes take longer. Scoop the tomatoes out of the boiling water and plunge them into the ice water to prevent the outer layer of flesh from cooking and softening. Remove from the water, and use a paring knife to cut out the cores at the stem end and slip off the skins.

To seed the tomatoes, cut them in half horizontally, use your fingers to loosen the seeds in their cavities, and squeeze the halves to coax the seeds out. Work over a bowl with a strainer to catch the delicious juice. Once peeled and seeded, the tomatoes are ready to be stuffed and baked, diced or chopped for any number of preparations, or sliced and dressed for a salad.

SIMPLE TOMATO SAUCE
MAKES ABOUT 4 CUPS

I like an uncomplicated tomato sauce that tastes of sweet, flavorful tomatoes, garlic, and chile. It makes a delicious pasta sauce by itself, or it can be garnished with fresh herbs and cheese, and it can be the base of many other sauces.

4 pounds ripe tomatoes, or two 28-ounce cans peeled whole tomatoes	½ cup olive oil
	2 bay leaves
	Dried chile flakes
8 to 10 garlic cloves	Salt

Peel, seed, and chop the fresh tomatoes, or seed and chop the canned tomatoes; reserve the juice. Peel and chop the garlic. Put the oil in a heavy-bottomed pot over medium heat and add the garlic. When the garlic begins to sizzle and release its fragrance, add the tomatoes and juice, bay leaves, a big pinch of chile flakes, and salt. Simmer the sauce for 20 minutes or so, until thickened. Remove the bay leaves and taste for seasoning; add more salt and chile flakes to taste. (If the tomatoes are too acidic and not as sweet as you would like, add a bit of sugar.) For a smooth sauce, pass through a food mill.

RAW TOMATO SOUP

4 SERVINGS

Charlie makes this refreshing soup when tomatoes are at their peak of ripeness and flavor. The same method can be applied to extract flavor from other watery vegetables and fruits, such as cucumber and watermelon.

8 medium to large ripe tomatoes
Salt
8 ounces cherry tomatoes
1 crisp medium cucumber,
   thinly sliced

Fresh-ground black pepper
Olive oil
A few sprigs of herbs, such as
   basil, dill, marjoram, or mint

Wash the tomatoes and cut out the cores. Cut the tomatoes into pieces and sprinkle with salt—the salt flavors the tomatoes and helps release the juice. Put the tomatoes and any juice through a food mill into a bowl. Put a sieve over a bowl, line the sieve with a piece of cheesecloth, and pour the tomato pulp remaining in the food mill into it. Gather up the cheesecloth, twist it closed, and squeeze the juice from the pulp into the bowl.

Cut the cherry tomatoes into halves or quarters, and combine with the cucumber. Season with salt and pepper and moisten with olive oil. Strip the leaves off the herb sprigs, chop them fine, and add to the cherry tomatoes and cucumber. Divide this mixture among 4 bowls and spoon over the tomato juice. Finish with a drizzle of olive oil and serve.

TOMATOES BAKED WITH BREADCRUMBS

Small sweet tomatoes, either peeled or unpeeled, are excellent stuffed with breadcrumbs and garlic, then baked. Make a mixture of fresh breadcrumbs (page 40), chopped garlic, and chopped basil; the proportions of the stuffing can vary; I like it with lots of garlic. Core the tomatoes and cut them in half horizontally. Loosen the seeds and squeeze them out. Season the tomatoes with salt and pepper, and fill the seed cavities with the breadcrumb mixture. Preheat the oven to 375°F. Fit the tomatoes in a single layer in a gratin dish and drizzle olive oil over each one. Bake for 20 to 30 minutes, until nicely browned.

LIDIA BASTIANICH is one of my favorite cooking teachers on television. Her style is briskly matter-of-fact and down-to-earth; she never performs, she simply demonstrates. She is revitalizing our understanding of Italian food with her reliance on local ingredients and straightforward technique, and she personifies all that is good about cooking within a tradition.

« BOILING PASTA »

It's a good idea to always have on hand a few kinds of dried pasta and egg noodles for an impromptu supper. Whatever the shape or type, noodles and pasta cook best in a large pot of boiling salted water so they won't stick together as they cook. Cook pasta al dente (to the tooth)—cooked through, with no white core at the center, but still firm, not flabby. Thin pastas like spaghettini and delicate egg noodles cook quickly and are often best when removed from the water while still undercooked and allowed to finish cooking in a pan of sauce. Thicker pastas take longer and there is less danger of overcooking. Drain the pasta when it is done, but always save some of the cooking water—it is very tasty and useful to add to the pasta and sauce if it is a little thick and needs loosening.

SPAGHETTINI WITH GARLIC, PARSLEY & OLIVE OIL
2 SERVINGS

This dish of Lidia's is what I make for supper when I return home tired and hungry after traveling. I like it very plain, with lots of parsley, but you could spice it up by adding a pinch of dried chile flakes or chopped anchovy, and serving it with grated cheese.

Salt

⅓ pound spaghettini

2 to 3 tablespoons olive oil

2 garlic cloves, peeled and thinly sliced

8 to 10 branches Italian parsley,
    stems removed, leaves chopped

Bring a generous pot of salted water to a boil over high heat, and stir in the spaghettini. Stir frequently and cook for 5 to 6 minutes, until tender but still firm.

Meanwhile, put the olive oil and garlic in a saucepan and heat gently until the garlic begins to sizzle and release its fragrance; take care that it does not brown or burn. Add the parsley to the pan along with ½ cup of the pasta water. When the pasta is cooked, use a skimmer to lift it out of the water and directly into the pan, or drain it, reserving some of the water, and then add to the pan. Toss the pasta and let it simmer briefly in the sauce to finish cooking and absorb the flavors; add more pasta water if needed to keep the pasta loose and saucy. Taste the pasta for salt, and add more if needed. Serve immediately in warm bowls.

WHOLE-WHEAT SPAGHETTI WITH KALE
4 SERVINGS

Kale is a strong-flavored green that is both bitter and sweet—Red Russian and lacinato varieties are especially good—and combined with garlic, dried chile flakes, and nutty wheat spaghetti, kale makes a bold and satisfying pasta dish.

1½ pounds kale, about 2 bunches	1 large onion, peeled and thinly sliced
Salt	A large pinch of dried chile flakes
1 pound whole-wheat spaghetti	4 garlic cloves, peeled and chopped
½ cup olive oil	Parmesan or Romano cheese

Remove the tough stems from the kale leaves. Discard the stems, and coarsely chop the greens. Rinse the kale and drain. Bring a large pot of water to a boil, and season with a generous amount of salt. Add the spaghetti and cook until al dente, tender but still firm.

While the pasta cooks, heat a large, heavy sauté pan over medium-high heat. Add about half the oil, the onion, chili flakes, and a pinch of salt, and cook, stirring occasionally, until the onion is tender and lightly colored, about 5 to 7 minutes. (If the onion begins to scorch, reduce the heat to medium.) Add the kale and cook, stirring and tossing, until the kale is wilted and tender, about 3 minutes. Add water to the pan if the greens are dry, and if the greens are on the sturdy side, cover the pan briefly to steam them. Add the garlic, season with salt, and cook for 2 minutes more. Take care that the garlic does not brown.

Drain the pasta when cooked, reserving some of the pasta water. Add the pasta to the sauté pan and toss to combine. Loosen with a splash of the cooking water if needed, and taste for salt. Transfer the pasta to a warm platter or serving bowls, and drizzle a thin stream of olive oil on top. Garnish with shavings of Parmesan or Romano cheese, and serve immediately.

» Use other greens in place of the kale: broccoli rabe (rapini), chard, beet greens, or turnip greens. Adjust the cooking time depending on the maturity and tenderness of the greens.
» Finish the sautéed kale with a squeeze of lemon juice or a splash of red wine vinegar, and garnish the pasta with shavings of ricotta salata cheese.
» Use only 3 tablespoons of olive oil and add ¼ pound of diced pancetta to the pan before adding the onion. Cook the pancetta until it is lightly browned, but not crisp. Remove the pancetta from the pan and set aside. Continue the recipe as directed, and return the pancetta to the pan when you add the pasta.

LINGUINE WITH CLAMS

4 SERVINGS

When using smaller clams such as Manila and littleneck, make this pasta with the clams in their shells. When using larger clams, cook them first, remove from their shells, and chop, returning them to the pot with the tasty clam liquor.

2 pounds small clams
Salt
1 pound linguine
5 tablespoons olive oil
1 carrot, peeled and finely diced
1 onion, peeled and finely diced

1 celery stalk, finely diced
5 or 6 garlic cloves, peeled and
   finely chopped
A large pinch of dried chile flakes
½ cup white wine
1 tablespoon chopped Italian parsley

Wash the clams well under running water. If they are sandy, soak them in a large bowl of water for 30 minutes or so. Drain well.

Heat a large pot of salted water to boiling, and add the linguine. Stir and cook until al dente, tender but still firm.

Heat a heavy-bottomed pan over medium-high heat. Add 1 tablespoon of the olive oil to the pan, and add the carrot, onion, and celery (mirepoix; see page 138). Cook briefly to soften the mirepoix, then add the clams, garlic, chile flakes, and white wine. Cover the pan and cook until the clams open, 6 to 7 minutes. When the clams have opened, add the parsley and the remaining 4 tablespoons olive oil.

When the pasta is cooked, drain and add it to the pan with the clams, and toss with the clam sauce. Taste for salt; some clams are very salty and some are mild. Add salt if needed. Serve immediately.

» Instead of white wine, add to the pot along with the clams ½ to ¾ cup Simple Tomato Sauce (page 53), or the same amount of diced fresh tomatoes.
» Substitute mussels for clams. Rinse them well and pull off the beards before cooking.
» In addition to or in place of the mirepoix, add a small bulb of fennel finely diced.
» Add a pinch of saffron threads to the pot with the clams and finish with ½ cup cream when the clams have opened.

POPPY TOOKER is a leader of Slow Food (whose symbol is a snail) and a fiercely loyal native of New Orleans who is playing a major role in the preservation and restoration of that city's food heritage in the aftermath of Hurricane Katrina. She is a passionate supporter of rare and disappearing food ways everywhere, and produced and hosted a television series about Slow Food's Ark of Taste called *Eat It to Save It*.

« COOKING RICE »

Cooking plain rice is not mysterious or difficult; it's as easy as boiling water. A time-honored New Orleans method of measuring the rice and water is to use your finger instead of a measuring cup, as below, but either way, the basic rule applies: 1 part long-grain rice and 2 parts water. Long-grain rice, such as basmati, will be drier and fluffier if it is washed and rinsed before cooking to remove the surface starch from the grains.

To prepare 4 to 6 servings of rice, select a 1- to 1½-quart saucepan with a tight-fitting lid. Place your index finger on the bottom of the pan and pour in long-grain white rice until it reaches the first joint of your finger. Still using your finger for measurement, pour water into the pan until it reaches the second joint of your index finger. Or measure 1½ cups rice and 3 cups water. If you like, add a pinch of salt and a pat of butter.

Place the pan over high heat and bring the water and rice to a full rolling boil. As soon as the water boils, cover the saucepan and reduce the heat to the lowest setting. Cook the rice undisturbed for 20 minutes. Remove the pan from the heat, use a fork to fluff up the grains of rice, and serve. If not serving right away, replace the cover to keep warm until ready.

» To cook short-grain white rice, use 1½ cups rice and 1¾ cups water. Bring the rice and water to a boil, then cover and cook over low heat for 15 minutes. Turn off the heat and let the rice rest, covered, for another 10 minutes.

» To cook short-grain brown rice, use 1½ cups rice and 3 cups water. Rinse the rice, bring the rice and water to a boil, stir and reduce the heat to low, and cover. Simmer for 50 minutes or until all the water is absorbed. Let stand, covered, for 10 minutes, then fluff with a fork and serve.

» Using a rice cooker is a foolproof way to cook and hold rice. Organic brown rice is nutty and delicious cooked with aromatic spices such as a cinnamon stick, whole cardamom seeds, bay leaves, black peppercorns, and salt.

DIRTY RICE

4 SERVINGS

Dirty rice is a spicy Cajun dish typically made with sausage, chicken giblets, and vegetables—the meats color the rice and make it look "dirty." There are as many versions of the dish as there are cooks. This one, contributed by Tanya Holland of Brown Sugar Kitchen, in Oakland, California, is spicy, light, and meatless.

2 tablespoons vegetable oil
1 green bell pepper, seeded and diced
1 red bell pepper, seeded and diced
1 jalapeño pepper, seeded and
    finely diced
1 onion, peeled and finely diced
3 garlic cloves, peeled and chopped
¼ cup Worcestershire sauce
3 cups cooked long-grain white or
    brown rice

1 tablespoon chopped parsley
1 tablespoon chopped thyme
1 teaspoon salt
1 teaspoon fresh-ground black
    pepper
½ teaspoon paprika
¼ teaspoon cayenne pepper
½ cup sliced green onions

Heat a large skillet over medium heat, add the oil to the pan followed by the peppers, onion, and garlic. Cook the vegetables until tender, about 10 minutes. Add the Worcestershire sauce and the rice. Stir to mix the rice evenly with the vegetables and sauce. Add the herbs, salt, black pepper, paprika, cayenne, and green onions. Lower the heat and cook gently for 10 to 15 minutes more. Taste and, if needed, add more salt before serving.

» Cut the kernels from 1 or 2 ears of corn and add to the rice with the seasonings and green onions. If you like, add a diced tomato as well.

SAFFRON RICE

4 SERVINGS

1 cup basmati rice
1½ teaspoons salt
1 tablespoon unsalted butter
A pinch of saffron threads, lightly toasted

Rinse the rice under cool water until the water runs clear. Bring 2 cups of water to a boil in a medium saucepan, and add the salt. Add the rice to the boiling water, and continue to boil, uncovered, for 6 minutes, stirring occasionally. Drain well, and return the rice to the pot. Add the butter and 3 tablespoons of water, cover tightly, and cook over low heat for 20 minutes. Turn off the heat and let the rice sit for 10 minutes.

Meanwhile, pound the saffron threads to a powder using a mortar and pestle. Add 2 teaspoons hot water and stir to combine. Remove ⅓ cup of the rice from the pan and put it in a small bowl. Add the saffron water to the rice and stir until the rice is stained yellow. (Or if your mortar is large enough, add the rice directly to the saffron water in the mortar.) There shouldn't be any excess liquid. If there is, pour off the liquid. Return the rice to the pan, and stir gently to fluff and combine the white and golden grains of rice.

» Alternatively, add the pounded saffron to the pot along with the butter, rather than making a saffron-infused water. This way, the rice will be evenly yellow, as opposed to a mixture of white and golden grains of rice.
» Add ⅓ cup golden raisins or currants to the rice along with the butter, and stir in ⅓ cup chopped toasted almonds or toasted pine nuts just before serving.

DAVID TANIS spends half the year as chef of the downstairs restaurant at Chez Panisse and the other half in Paris cooking for small crowds of friends in his tiny galley kitchen, with its less-than-adequate stove, toylike refrigerator, and nearly total lack of counter space. These deficiencies do not appear to trouble him in the least. His latest book is *A Platter of Figs and Other Recipes.*

« SIMMERING BEANS »

Cooking dried beans is as basic as it gets: put the beans in a pot, cover with water, and simmer until tender. What varies around the globe is the variety of bean and how they are seasoned. There are many heirloom varieties to choose from and they are all delicious flavored with a mirepoix (a mixture of diced or chopped onions, carrot, and celery) and a few herbs, and if you like, a bit of cured meat. Cook beans that you intend to add to a soup or some other dish with whole, not chopped, vegetables and remove them at the end.

WHITE BEANS WITH GARLIC & HERBS
6 TO 8 SERVINGS

1 pound dried cannellini beans, cranberry, or other dried beans
Olive oil
1 onion, peeled and diced
1 carrot, peeled and diced
1 celery stalk, diced
4 garlic cloves, peeled and chopped

1 bay leaf
1 or 2 sprigs thyme, sage, savory, or rosemary
Ham hock, or a piece of pancetta or bacon (optional)
Salt

Rinse the beans and pick over, removing any small stones or debris. If time allows, soak the beans, covered by an inch or so of water, for several hours or overnight. (Otherwise, proceed without soaking the beans first.) Cover the bottom of a large heavy pot or earthenware bean pot with olive oil, add the vegetables and herbs, and cook gently over medium heat for 10 minutes. Drain the beans and add to the pot along with enough water to cover by 2 inches. If you like, add a ham hock or other meat to the pot.

Bring the beans to a boil, and let them boil for a minute or two. Lower the heat to a very gentle simmer and cook the beans until tender, 1 to 2 hours, depending on their variety and age. Add more hot water as needed during the cooking to keep the beans covered by at least an inch of water. When the beans are soft, add salt, taste after a few minutes, and add more salt if needed.

Serve the beans moistened with the cooking broth and, if you like, a drizzle of olive oil. If not serving right away, let the beans cool completely in the broth, and refrigerate. They will keep for 3 or 4 days in the refrigerator.

FRESH SHELL BEANS
4 SERVINGS

Fresh shell beans are superb. A bowl of plump shell beans flavored with only olive oil, black pepper, and salt, with a glass of wine, and some crusty bread—that's food for the gods, as David says. All sorts of varieties—cranberry, cannellini, flageolet, lima, and butter beans, crowder peas and black-eyed peas—are harvested in the summer and fall, and are becoming more common in farmers' markets. Fresh beans will cook in 30 to 45 minutes.

3 pounds fresh cranberry or
    cannellini beans in the pod
    (about 3 cups shelled beans)
Olive oil
Salt

1 bay leaf
A few sage leaves or a sprig
    of rosemary or thyme
Fresh-ground black pepper

Shell the beans. Put them in a large heavy pot or an earthenware bean pot, and cover with water by 2 inches. Add a splash of olive oil, a good pinch of salt, the bay leaf, and the sage leaves or sprig of rosemary or thyme. Bring to a boil, reduce to a simmer, and cook gently for 30 to 45 minutes, until tender throughout. Turn off the heat, and let the beans cool down in the broth. Reheat gently when ready to serve. Pour off most of the broth (save it for soup or some other use), season the beans with salt and black pepper, and drizzle with olive oil.

» One of my favorite pastas is made with shell beans. Gently heat olive oil, chopped garlic, and chopped rosemary or sage. Add cooked beans and some of their broth, stew briefly, and mash about half the beans to make a loose thick sauce. Cook dried pasta (bucatini or strozzapreti are two good kinds) and stir into the beans; loosen with pasta water or bean broth if needed. Add chopped wilted greens, if you like, and garnish with fresh-ground pepper and olive oil.
» Cooked beans can be combined with other vegetables to make hearty soups (see the recipe that follows); served warm or as salads with green beans, wilted greens, mushrooms, or tomatoes; baked in gratins; served with roasted meats and the meat juices; or warmed with olive oil, garlic, and herbs and mashed into a purée to spread on garlic croutons (see page 37).

SHELL BEAN & VEGETABLE SOUP

4 TO 6 SERVINGS

I make this soup year-round with fresh shell beans in the summer and fall, and with dried beans in the winter. The other vegetables in the soup vary with the season. It can be put together quickly if the beans are already cooked.

3 tablespoons olive oil
1 onion, peeled and diced
1 large carrot, peeled and diced
1 celery stalk, diced
2 garlic cloves, peeled and chopped
2 thyme sprigs
2 bay leaves
Salt
3 cups liquid (bean broth, water, or chicken stock, or any combination of the three)
2 small summer squash, diced

8 ounces green beans, trimmed and cut into 1-inch pieces
½ bunch chard leaves, coarsely chopped
3 cups cooked cannellini, cranberry, or other beans
1 large tomato, peeled, seeded, and chopped
Garlic croutons (see page 37; optional)
Parmesan cheese

Heat the olive oil in a large heavy pot over medium heat and add the onion, carrot, and celery. Cook the vegetables gently for 5 to 10 minutes until soft and translucent. Add the garlic and herbs, season with salt, and cook another few minutes. Add the liquid and bring to a simmer. Add the squash, green beans, and chard (or other vegetables in season, such as leeks, fennel, winter squash, kale, cabbage, and potatoes). Simmer until the vegetables are tender, 10 to 15 minutes. Add the cooked shell beans and the tomato and cook for another 5 minutes. Taste and add salt and more liquid, if needed. Serve the soup with a drizzle of olive oil and, if you like, a plate of crusty garlic croutons to dip into the broth. Pass Parmesan at the table.

» A classic minestrone includes pasta in the soup (add 1 to 2 cups cooked pasta, such as orzo or orecchiette, to the soup at the end) and is garnished at the table with a generous spoonful of pesto (page 21) added to each bowl. The pesto gives a pungent garlicky kick to the soup, in which case you won't need the olive oil and cheese of the original recipe as a garnish.
» For a winter version of the soup, substitute cubes of winter squash (butternut, Hubbard, pumpkin) for the summer squash and green beans, and use kale in place of the chard. Use canned or preserved tomatoes in place of the fresh to-matoes, or leave them out.

Fava Bean Purée

Fresh fava beans have an extraordinary flavor like no other bean. The early beans of spring are small and tender, and a delicacy in soups, salads, and pastas. Larger, more mature and starchy favas are better suited to longer cooking and make a brilliant green purée to spread on croutons.

Fava beans require a little extra effort to shell and peel before cooking, but they are well worth it. First they must be stripped from the large green spongy pods, and then each bean needs to be peeled to remove the skin.

2 to 3 pounds fava beans in the pod
About ½ cup olive oil
½ cup water
Salt

3 garlic cloves, peeled and chopped
1 to 2 teaspoons chopped rosemary
Fresh-ground black pepper

Shell the beans, and heat a pot of water to boiling. Blanch the beans briefly (for 30 seconds or so) to loosen the skins; drain and cool in ice water, to preserve their bright green color. Peel the beans: Use your thumbnail to tear the skin at one end, then squeeze to pop out the bean.

Heat about ¼ cup of the olive oil in a heavy-bottomed saucepan and add the beans, the water, and a generous pinch of salt. Cook the beans gently, stirring occasionally, for 10 to 15 minutes, until very soft. Add more water if needed to keep them moist and loose. Mash the beans to a paste with a wooden spoon or potato masher. Make a well in the center of the pan and pour in another few tablespoons of the olive oil. Add the garlic and rosemary to the oil and cook gently; when the garlic starts to sizzle and releases its fragrance, stir the mixture into the beans. Season with a few grinds of pepper. Taste and add more salt, olive oil, or water as needed.

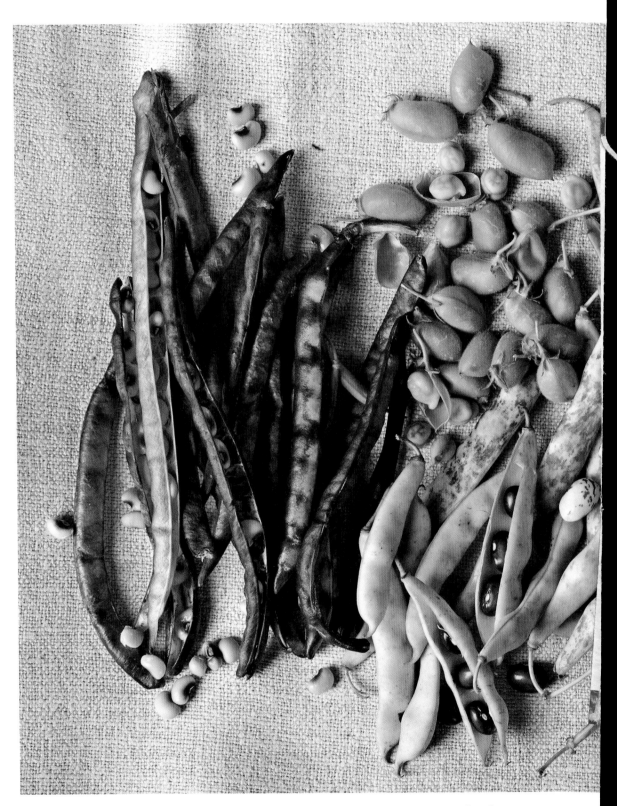

Left to right: black-eyed peas; (top) chick peas; coco negro beans; cranberry beans; (top) yellow beans; romano beans; green filet beans.

NILOUFER ICHAPORIA KING was born in Bombay and now resides in San Francisco with her husband and her parrot. She is the author of *My Bombay Kitchen*, an endearing and authoritative introduction to the great cuisine of India's disappearing Parsi minority. She applies an anthropologist's curiosity to her study of food ways around the world, particularly those of the tropics, and she has a magic touch with greens.

« WILTING GREENS »

Leafy greens of all sorts are good simply wilted, cooked by a combination of steaming and sautéing. Tender greens such as spinach, watercress, and pea shoots cook quickly, in just a few minutes, uncovered. The sturdier greens (chard, kale, broccoli rabe, collards, cabbage, amaranth, beet greens, turnip tops) take longer. These are best cut into ribbons, or shreds, and covered to steam during cooking. It helps to have a large shallow pan that can accommodate a big mound of leaves at the outset, a tight-fitting lid, and a pair of tongs to stir and lift the greens to keep them moving and cooking evenly.

GREENS WITH GINGER & CHILE
4 SERVINGS

1 to 1½ pounds amaranth or other leafy greens
4 coin-size slices peeled fresh ginger
1 to 2 tablespoons oil

Salt
1 fresh red or green chile, or 1 dried red chile

Sort the greens, removing any tough stems, and wash and drain the leaves. Cut the ginger slices into a fine julienne, or chop them, or simply leave them as round slices. Cover the bottom of a wok or generous skillet with a layer of oil, and heat over medium-high heat. Add some salt to the oil, then add the ginger and the chile pod. Any number of kinds of chile will do; it is for flavor, not heat. If it is a fresh chile, make a slit in it to prevent it from bursting in the heat. When the ginger begins to sizzle, stir it around and add the greens. Use tongs to toss the greens to distribute the oil and flavorings and to keep the greens moving and cooking evenly. Very tender greens will wilt and cook in 1 to 2 minutes. For sturdier greens, reduce the heat and cover the pan for a few minutes to let them steam and wilt. The greens are delicious served warm or at room temperature.

OLIVER ROWE is another young chef with international experience who has made a dramatic return to his local roots: A Londoner by birth, a few years ago he opened his restaurant, Konstam at the Prince Albert, in a neighborhood where he has strong family ties. A fanatic for local food, he obtains over 80 percent of his ingredients from producers within the area served by the London Underground.

« BLANCHING GREENS »

Oliver likes to blanch his greens. Blanching vegetables means cooking them briefly in rapidly boiling water. Blanching is suitable for all sorts of leafy greens: chard, kale, beet greens, turnip tops, collards, cabbage, spinach, sea purslane, dandelion, and nettles. Blanched greens can be seasoned and served warm; chopped and added to stuffings, meatballs, soups, and stews; or dressed and served cold or at room temperature.

RAINBOW CHARD WITH OIL & GARLIC
4 SERVINGS

1 large bunch rainbow chard
Salt
2 garlic cloves
Olive oil

Separate the ribs and leaves of the chard; they cook at different rates. Cut the leaves into broad ribbons and cut the ribs into 1-inch pieces. Heat a large pot of water to boiling and salt it generously—there should be enough salt in the water to permeate the greens and bring out their flavor. Taste the water; it should be as salty as seawater. Have a large bowl of ice water ready for refreshing the greens.

Cook the chard leaves in the boiling water for 1 minute or so, until wilted. Lift the leaves out with a large strainer and immediately plunge them into the ice water, which stops the cooking so that the chard stays bright green. Next, blanch the ribs, cooking them until tender, 4 to 5 minutes. Transfer them to the ice water with the leaves and when cool enough to handle, drain, gather handfuls, and squeeze out the excess water.

Peel the garlic and cut into slivers. Over low heat, warm some olive oil in a pan, add the garlic, and cook gently until fragrant and soft. Add the chard and cook, stirring, until it has warmed through. Season with salt and serve.

» Try flavoring blanched greens with various combinations of lemon or vinegar, garlic, ginger, chile, pancetta or bacon, and anchovy. Combine greens with other vegetables such as shell beans, onions, and squash; or add them to dishes such as frittatas, gratins, soups, and pastas.

DAN BARBER, chef and co-owner of the Blue Hill restaurants in New York, is one of our most influential advocates for sustainable agriculture and a healthier food system. He addresses food issues in essays and op-ed pieces written from his unique perspective as a chef whose ingredients come from his own farm, Blue Hill, in Great Barrington, Massachusetts, and Stone Barns Center for Food and Agriculture, a not-for-profit farm and education center with a mission to celebrate, teach, and advance community-based food production.

« STEAMING VEGETABLES »

Steaming is one of the simplest and most nutritious ways to cook vegetables. It is an especially good method to capture the delicate flavors of tender young vegetables such as turnips and turnip greens, carrots and carrot tops, peas and pea shoots, green beans, cauliflower, beets, and spinach. After cooking, the vegetables can be seasoned lightly with salt and perhaps a squeeze of lemon juice, or flavored with various vinegars, olive oil or butter, or a sauce.

CAULIFLOWER WITH PARSLEY & VINEGAR
4 SERVINGS

2 small or 1 medium cauliflower
Salt and fresh-ground black pepper
Red wine vinegar
Olive oil

Leaves of 10 to 12 sprigs Italian
  parsley, chopped
½ cup toasted breadcrumbs (page 40)

Cut out the core of each cauliflower and separate the head into florets; cut large florets into 2 or 3 pieces to make them about the same size as the smaller whole florets. Place a steamer basket in a saucepan with a tight-fitting lid, pour in water to a level just below the bottom of the basket, and heat the water to boiling. Add the cauliflower to the basket and cook, covered, for 6 to 8 minutes, until the stalks are just tender when pierced with a knife. Remove the basket from the pan and transfer the cauliflower to a bowl. Season the florets with salt and fresh-ground pepper, sprinkle lightly with vinegar and oil to taste, and stir in the parsley. Serve warm topped with breadcrumbs, or chill and serve as a salad.

Steamed Tokyo Turnips

Tokyo turnips are a beautiful all-white variety that are sweet tasting and mildly spicy. When harvested young, about 1 inch in diameter, the smooth skins are thin and delicate and don't need to be peeled. At that stage, the greens are tender and small, and both turnips and greens are good for steaming. If the greens and turnips are in pristine condition, they are very good steamed whole with the greens attached. Otherwise, separate the turnips and greens, leaving an inch or so of the pale green stalks at the top of the turnips. Rinse the turnips well to remove any grit in the stalks, and leave them whole or cut into halves or quarters. Wash the greens and discard any yellow or damaged leaves. Place a steamer basket in a saucepan with a tight-fitting lid, pour in water to a depth of half an inch or so, and heat the water to boiling. Add the turnips and greens to the basket, cover the pan, and cook until just tender, 5 to 8 minutes, depending on their size. They are delicious eaten with nothing more than a little salt and butter or a drizzle of olive oil, or with a dash of vinegar or soy sauce, or a squeeze of lemon juice.

BUTTERED COUSCOUS
4 TO 6 SERVINGS

Couscous, made of semolina wheat rolled into tiny granules, is the traditional dish of Morocco and northern Africa. It is cooked to a light and fluffy texture by steaming it several times, perfumed by the aromatic spices in the steamer. It is usually paired with meat or vegetable stews—try it with Moroccan-Style Braised Vegetables (page 111)—and with spicy harissa sauce (page 112). There are instant varieties available, but cooking it the traditional way results in the best texture and flavor.

1½ cups couscous
Salt
1 tablespoon cumin seeds
1 tablespoon coriander seeds
1 teaspoon ground turmeric
2 garlic cloves, peeled and chopped

One 1½-inch piece of fresh ginger, peeled and coarsely chopped
A few sprigs of cilantro
2 lemon leaves (optional)
2 tablespoons butter, melted

Put the couscous in a colander and rinse thoroughly with cool water. Drain well and spread out in a large shallow pan. Season lightly with salt. Let the couscous swell for 15 minutes, then rub your fingers through the couscous to break up any lumps.

Set up a steamer: Bring 8 cups of water to a boil in the bottom of the steamer. Add the cumin, coriander, turmeric, garlic, ginger, cilantro, and lemon leaves (a fragrant addition if you have access to a lemon tree). Reduce the heat to maintain a brisk boil. Transfer the couscous to the steamer basket (if the holes in the steamer basket are large, line the basket with damp cheesecloth), cover tightly, and steam for 20 minutes.

Transfer the couscous back to the shallow pan and moisten with ½ cup of water. Using a spoon or your hands, fluff the grains and break up any lumps. Let the couscous rest for 15 minutes at room temperature, then return it to the steamer, and steam for another 20 minutes. Drizzle with the melted butter, and fluff the grains once more. Taste for salt, and serve.

The couscous can sit for some time before the final steaming. Cover it with a damp clean dish towel to keep it moist, and break up any lumps before returning it to the steamer.

DAVID CHANG has several New York restaurants that serve what you might call slow fast food: food eaten at a counter that is both delicious and absolutely right for the occasion. His inspirations are global, and he honors his Korean background by creating imaginative and unexpected dishes that combine classic Western ingredients and techniques with the purest of Asian flavors.

« PICKLING VEGETABLES »

Freshly pickled vegetables make colorful, tasty appetizers and lively condiments for sandwiches, cold meat plates, or fried foods. One of the pleasures of pickling vegetables is cutting and slicing them to show off their beautiful shapes and colors—especially winter root vegetables. Vinegar pickles (page 82), as well as vegetables briefly cured with only salt and sugar, can be prepared and served right away, or chilled and served later.

SALT & SUGAR PICKLES
4 SERVINGS

David makes these pickles to be enjoyed right after seasoning, while they are still vibrant and crunchy.

3 very large radishes

2 thin daikon radishes

2 thin-skinned cucumbers with
   few seeds

2 pounds seedless watermelon

1 teaspoon fine sea salt

1 teaspoon sugar

Prepare the vegetables and fruit and arrange in separate bowls; there should be about 1½ cups of each kind. Halve the radishes and slice into thin wedges. Cut the daikon radishes crosswise into slices about ⅛ inch thick. Cut the cucumbers crosswise into slices about ¼ inch thick. Remove the rind of the watermelon and cut the flesh into slices ⅓ inch thick and then into 2-inch wedges.

In a small bowl, combine the salt and sugar, and sprinkle ½ teaspoon of the mixture over each vegetable and the watermelon and toss. Let the pickles stand for 5 to 10 minutes, arrange separately on a platter, and serve immediately.

Vinegar Pickles

4 SERVINGS

A basic fresh pickling method is to make a brine, bring it to a boil, and cook cut-up vegetables in the simmering liquid until they are just tender, but still a bit crisp. Many vegetables are good for pickling; prepare as many different kinds as you like, but cook them separately.

1½ cups white wine vinegar
1½ cups water
2½ tablespoons sugar
1 teaspoon salt
1 bay leaf
2 or 3 sprigs thyme
½ teaspoon coriander seeds

2 whole cloves
1 dried cayenne pepper or a pinch
    dried chile flakes
Assorted vegetables: carrots, fennel,
    turnips, cauliflower and broccoli
    florets, onions, green beans, okra,
    beets

Combine the vinegar, water, sugar, salt, herbs, spices, and pepper in a nonreactive saucepan, bring to a boil, then lower the heat to a simmer. Prepare assorted vegetables by peeling, if needed, and trimming and cutting them into same-size shapes—quartered small turnips, sliced fennel, whole or halved small carrots, sliced beets. Because cooking times will vary, cook the different vegetables separately in the simmering brine. Let cool and serve at room temperature, or chill.

A similar method for especially tender young vegetables such as carrots, radishes, fennel, and turnips is to macerate, not cook, them in the brine. Heat the brine to boiling, then let it cool to room temperature. Soak the vegetables separately for 30 to 60 minutes, until they are flavored through yet still retain their crunchy freshness, drain, then chill to further crisp and refresh them.

FRIED FISH WITH PICKLED VEGETABLES
4 SERVINGS

Tangy and crunchy fresh vegetable pickles are a perfect foil to fried fish. They cut the richness of the buttery breadcrumbs and make a beautiful and colorful plate. This method of breading and cooking the fish is also excellent for chicken breasts.

4 fish fillets (sole, halibut, or other
  firm white-fleshed fish; about
  5 ounces each)
Salt and fresh-ground black pepper
½ cup all-purpose flour

1 egg
2 cups fresh breadcrumbs (page 40)
6 tablespoons (¾ stick) unsalted
  clarified butter (see below)
Pickled vegetables (see opposite)

Season the fish fillets with salt and pepper. Put the following separately into 3 shallow bowls: the flour, the egg beaten with a tablespoon of water, and the breadcrumbs. One fillet at a time, dredge the fish in the flour and shake off the excess, dip in the beaten egg, and finally roll or pat in the breadcrumbs. Refrigerate the fillets for at least 30 minutes to dry the breadcrumb coating.

Heat a cast-iron skillet or other heavy pan over medium heat and add the butter. (To quickly clarify butter, melt it in a small saucepan and skim off the milk solids that float to the top; the milk solids will burn at frying temperatures.) When the butter is bubbling, add the fillets and cook until the bottoms are browned and crisp, 3 to 4 minutes. Turn and cook on the other side until nicely browned and crisp. Remove from the pan and drain briefly on a clean dish towel; serve with a variety of fresh pickles.

CAL PETERNELL has been one of the Chez Panisse Café co-chefs since 2000, and one of our strongest and most effective supporters of edible education. He grew up on a small New Jersey farm, and before he was seduced by food and wine he pursued a career in art. He continually surprises me with his inventive artist's eye.

« SKINNING PEPPERS »

Roasting and peeling peppers intensifies their natural sweetness and adds smoky, toasty flavors. They can be oven-roasted or charred over an open flame.

Choose ripe, sweet, thick-fleshed peppers and rub them with olive oil. Roast them in an earthenware dish or a roasting pan for 30 to 40 minutes in a 400°F oven, turning occasionally, until the skins are blistered and pulling away from the flesh. Remove the peppers from the oven and put them in a paper bag or a closed container so that they steam as they cool down. The steaming helps loosen the skins and makes it easier to slip off the skins with your hands. When peeled, slit the peppers open and lay them flat, cut side up, on a cutting board. Cut away the stem ends, and scrape out the membranes and seeds. Turn over and scrape away any remaining bits of charred skin.

Alternatively, peppers can be roasted over an open flame or under the broiler, or grilled over a hot charcoal fire. Keep a close eye on them and turn with tongs as the skins blister and blacken. Let cool, skin, and clean them as above.

ROASTED PEPPER SALAD
4 SERVINGS

This salad is especially good made with peppers roasted over a wood or charcoal fire.

3 or 4 thick-fleshed bell peppers
  or pimentos
1 garlic clove
1 tablespoon olive oil

1 teaspoon red wine vinegar
Salt and fresh-ground black pepper
Several sprigs of marjoram or basil
Garlic croutons (page 37; optional)

Roast, peel, and seed the peppers as directed above. Cut the peppers into strips. Peel the garlic and pound it to a purée in a mortar. Mix the garlic with the oil and vinegar, combine with the peppers, and season with salt and pepper to taste. Chop the marjoram leaves or cut the basil leaves into ribbons, and add to the peppers. Let the peppers marinate for a while for the flavors to come together. Serve as a salad on its own, as part of an antipasto plate, or with garlic croutons.

» If you like, spice up the salad with anchovy fillets, capers, mozzarella cheese, onion, or black olives.

PEPERONATA

4 SERVINGS

This is a dish of onion and sweet peppers cooked slowly until they are very soft and caramelized. It is a good filling for omelets or side dish for roasted meats.

1 large onion
3 or 4 large red or yellow bell peppers
Olive oil
Salt

Peel and slice the onion. Seed the peppers and cut them into 1-inch strips. Heat a large heavy skillet or sauté pan over medium heat, pour in olive oil to cover the bottom of the pan, and add the onion. Salt the onion and cook, stirring frequently, until it has softened and released its juice and reduced in volume, 20 to 30 minutes. Add water as needed if it becomes dry and sticks to the pan while cooking. When the onion is completely soft, turn up the heat and, stirring constantly, cook briefly to brown and caramelize it; take care that it does not burn. When the onion has browned, add about ½ cup water and stir to loosen the brown juice on the bottom of the pan.

Reduce the heat and add the peppers. Cook the peppers and onion, stirring frequently, until the peppers have begun to soften and wilt, about 15 minutes. Add a little water as needed if the vegetables begin to dry in the pan. Lower the heat and continue cooking the peperonata until it is meltingly soft, about 20 to 30 minutes. Turn off the heat and let the peperonata cool down. It is best served tepid or at room temperature.

GYPSY PEPPER & ONION SALAD

Sweet, thin-fleshed peppers, such as Gypsy, Lipstick, and other mild peppers, are delicious sliced thin and dressed as a raw salad. Choose a mixture of yellow, orange, and red peppers. Cut them in half lengthwise and remove the stems, membranes, and seeds. Cut the peppers lengthwise into very thin slices. Peel a red onion, cut in half lengthwise, and slice very thin (there should be about half as many onions as peppers). Combine the peppers and onion, and dress with salt, a splash of red wine vinegar, and olive oil. Peel and finely chop a garlic clove, or pound it to a paste in a mortar, and add it to the peppers and onion. Let the salad marinate a bit to soften, add some chopped herbs, if you like, and serve.

SAUTÉED WHOLE PEPPERS

Salty sautéed peppers, especially those that are mildly hot, are delicious summer treats—irresistible bites with a glass of chilled wine.

Cover the bottom of a sauté pan with a film of olive oil and put over medium heat. Add small, whole thin-fleshed peppers such as Lipstick and Nardello, or the small green Padrón pimentos (some are spicy and some are not), and cook, stirring frequently, for 5 to 10 minutes, until the peppers have softened and the skins have started to blister. Serve warm sprinkled with coarse sea salt.

BRYANT TERRY and ANNA LAPPÉ remind us that good food should be a right for everyone and not a privilege for a few. They are fighting for a system that will deliver food that is clean and safe to eat, and produced and marketed in ways that are fair to farmers, farm workers, and eaters alike. Bryant's latest book is *Vegan Soul Kitchen: Fresh, Healthy, and Creative African-American Cuisine;* Anna's is *Diet for a Hot Planet.*

« SHUCKING CORN »

For Bryant, shucking and eating freshly picked ears of corn reminds him how for generations his family was intimately connected with their food sources—they ate what they grew. When you eat juicy corn on the cob, served straight from the pot and slathered with butter, it's easy to imagine such a connection. Freshness really matters with corn—as soon as it is picked, the sugars in the corn start converting to starch. Choose ears that feel plump and fat with tightly closed, bright green husks and golden brown silks. Look for stems that are moist and pale green, and check for tight, small, plump kernels.

Kernels cut from the cob offer other possibilities: sautéed, with sweet peppers, chiles, tomatoes, squash, or beans; or used in cornbread and griddle cakes, and in numerous soups and salsas. To prepare kernels for cooking, pull off the husks and cornsilk from the ears of corn. Rub the ears with a clean dish towel to remove any clinging cornsilk, and snap off the stems. Cut the kernels from the cobs: Hold an ear by the tip, stand it up vertically with the stem end down, and use a sharp knife to cut down the length of the cob, cutting just deep enough to slice off the kernels. This is messy; to contain the kernels, it helps to work in a large bowl, or on a small cutting board set inside a roasting pan.

SAUTÉED JALAPEÑO CORN

4 SERVINGS

1 teaspoon cumin seeds	½ jalapeño pepper, chopped
Coarse salt	4 ears fresh corn, kernels cut off
Olive oil	the cobs (see above)
1 garlic clove, peeled and chopped	Fresh-ground black pepper

Toast the cumin seeds in a hot dry pan for a minute or so to bring out the fragrant oils, let cool a bit, then pulverize in a mortar along with a pinch of coarse salt.

Cover the bottom of a sauté pan with a coating of olive oil, put over medium heat, and add the garlic. (A tip to avoid burning garlic: Instead of adding chopped garlic to oil that may be too hot and will scorch it immediately, heat the garlic with the oil from the start, and you will see and hear it cooking gently and can prevent it from overheating.) When the garlic begins to sizzle, add the cumin and jalapeño and cook gently for another minute or so. Add the corn. Stir it while it cooks and, if needed, add a splash of water. The corn cooks quickly and will be done in 2 to 3 minutes. Finish with a few grinds of pepper and serve.

POLENTA WITH FRESH CORN

4 TO 6 SERVINGS

Polenta is ground corn cooked in water to make a thick and creamy porridge. Coarse, stone-ground dried corn makes delicious polenta and long, slow cooking allows its full flavor to develop. When hot and just cooked, it is soft; as it cools, it becomes firm and can then be cut into shapes and fried, grilled, or baked. Polenta is versatile; serve it with all kinds of roasted or braised meats and poultry, vegetable stews, tomato sauces and ragus, beans, mushrooms, and greens. This recipe adds the sweet taste and crunchy texture of fresh corn.

4 cups water
2½ teaspoons salt
1 cup coarse-ground polenta
2 ears fresh corn
3 tablespoons unsalted butter

In a heavy-bottomed pot, heat 4 cups water to boiling. Add the salt and whisk in the polenta, adding it in a steady thin stream. Turn down the heat and stir constantly until the polenta has thickened evenly. Cook at a bare simmer, stirring occasionally, for about 1 hour, until the polenta appears glossy and creamy. If the polenta gets too thick while cooking, add water to keep it a smooth, creamy consistency.

While the polenta cooks, prepare the fresh corn. Husk the corn and pull off the cornsilk; rub the ears with a clean dish towel to remove any remaining cornsilk. Cut the kernels from the cobs as directed on page 89. Heat a sauté pan over medium heat and add 2 tablespoons of the butter. When the butter has melted, add the corn and cook for about 5 minutes, until the kernels appear translucent; take care not to let it brown.

When the polenta is cooked, turn off the heat and stir in the cooked corn and remaining 1 tablespoon butter. Cover the pot to keep the polenta warm until ready to serve, or spread it out on a rimmed baking sheet or pan to cool and set up.

» In place of the corn, or in addition to it, add ½ cup grated fontina, pecorino, Gorgonzola, mascarpone, or Parmesan cheese.

CORNBREAD

6 TO 8 SERVINGS

A technique for making cornbread with an extra crispy crust is to bake it in a preheated cast-iron skillet. When fresh corn is in season, try adding juicy kernels to the batter.

1⅔ cups stone-ground cornmeal

1⅔ cups unbleached all-purpose flour

2½ tablespoons sugar

4 teaspoons baking powder

1½ teaspoons salt

2 eggs

½ cup plus 2 tablespoons vegetable oil or rendered good-quality lard

1⅔ cups milk

2 ears fresh corn (optional)

2 tablespoons unsalted butter

Position a rack in the middle of the oven, and preheat the oven to 375°F.

Put the cornmeal, flour, sugar, baking powder, and salt in a large bowl, and whisk to combine. In a small bowl, whisk together the eggs, oil, and milk. Add the egg mixture to the cornmeal mixture, and stir until just combined. If adding fresh corn to the batter: Husk the ears of corn, pull off the cornsilk, and cut the kernels from the cobs (see page 89); there should be about 2 cups. Stir the kernels into the batter.

Warm a heavy 10-inch ovenproof pan, preferably a cast-iron skillet, over medium-high heat. (A cast-iron pan produces a crispy brown crust, but you can also use a heavy nonstick pan.) Melt 1 tablespoon of the butter in the skillet, swirl to coat the pan, and add the batter. Put the pan in the oven and bake until the cornbread is golden brown on top and a toothpick inserted in the middle comes out clean, 35 to 40 minutes. Remove from the oven, let cool for a few minutes, then lift the cornbread out of the pan and transfer to a cooling rack. Rub the remaining 1 tablespoon butter on top. Allow the cornbread to cool for at least 5 minutes, then cut into wedges and serve.

» To make buttermilk cornbread, use 1¾ cups buttermilk instead of the milk.
» For a spicy cornbread, add chopped fresh chile peppers to the batter.

Clockwise from top left: Tiger Baby watermelon; yellow onions; saffron shallots; white corn; Armenian cucumber; Gypsy and Lipstick peppers.

DEBORAH MADISON lives on a ranch in New Mexico. Over the past twenty years, her cookbooks have become classics—the next best thing to having her by your side when you go to the farmers' market. She has changed the way we think about food, especially plant foods, with her inventive recipes and menus grounded in experience and elegantly thought through. She is a clear-eyed guide to locally grown food in season.

« ROASTING VEGETABLES »

Oven-roasting is an especially good way of cooking winter root vegetables such as potatoes, turnips, carrots, parsnips, and celery root, as well as onions, un-peeled garlic cloves, squashes, and fennel. The crispiness and caramelization that develops in the oven brings out the vegetables' natural sweetness and intensifies their flavors.

ROASTED POTATOES & TURNIPS
4 SERVINGS

3 or 4 medium potatoes
6 medium turnips
2 tablespoons olive oil

Salt and fresh-ground black pepper
Thyme, rosemary, sage, or bay leaves

Preheat the oven to 400°F. Peel the potatoes and turnips. Cut them into pieces about the same size and about ½ inch thick, so they will cook evenly. Toss the vegetables with a light coating of olive oil and season with salt and fresh-ground pepper. Sprinkle with chopped herbs or sprigs of herbs such as thyme, rosemary, sage, and bay leaves. Put the vegetables on a baking sheet or in a gratin dish and roast, stirring and turning the vegetables occasionally once they begin to color, until browned here and there and tender throughout, about 30 minutes. Take care not to overcook, or they can toughen and dry out.

» Add other vegetables, such as carrots, parsnips, rutabagas, winter squash, and fennel.
» While still hot from the oven, toss the vegetables with a mixture of finely chopped garlic and parsley.
» Eggplant is delicious roasted: Cut firm, shiny globe eggplant into slices about ½ inch thick. Brush the slices with olive oil on both sides, season with salt and fresh-ground pepper, and place on a baking sheet. Roast the eggplant at 400°F for 15 to 20 minutes, until the slices are nicely browned on the bottom. The slices will stick to the pan at first but will lift easily with a spatula once they are browned. Flip the slices over and cook for another 10 minutes or so, until browned on the other side. Keep an eye on them; the slices will cook faster on the second side.

POTATO GRATIN
6 SERVINGS

Earthenware dishes with a large surface area, that are shallow, low sided, and glazed on the inside, are perfect for slow-cooking in the oven and the formation of the golden crust of a gratin.

3 tablespoons butter
2¼ cups heavy cream
¾ cup chicken stock (page 47)
1 bay leaf
1 tablespoon kosher salt

4 pounds medium-size Yukon Gold
   or other waxy potatoes
1 tablespoon chopped thyme
Fresh-ground black pepper

Preheat the oven to 375°F. Butter a 14-inch oval gratin dish with 1 tablespoon of the butter. Put the cream, stock, bay leaf, and salt in a medium pot, and stir to combine. Bring the mixture to a simmer, reduce the heat to low, and let steep while you prepare the potatoes.

Peel the potatoes. Use a mandoline slicer or a knife to cut the potatoes into ⅛-inch-thick slices. Neatly layer the slices in the gratin dish, overlapping slightly, like shingles on a rooftop, making 3 or 4 layers. It's important to slice the potatoes and immediately assemble the gratin, before the potatoes oxidize and turn brown. Avoid putting the potatoes in water. You don't want to rinse off any of the potato starch—the starch is essential for a rich, creamy gratin.

Remove the bay leaf from the cream mixture and discard. Gently pour the mixture over the potatoes. The liquid level should be just below the surface of the potatoes; when you gently press the potatoes down with a spatula, the cream mixture should spill over the top layer of potatoes. Dot the remaining 2 tablespoons butter on top, and cover tightly with foil.

Bake until the potatoes are almost tender when pierced with a small, sharp knife, about 35 minutes. Increase the oven temperature to 400°F. Press the potatoes down with a spatula to an even thickness, allowing the creamy juices to baste the top. Sprinkle the thyme and black pepper on top. Continue to bake, uncovered, pressing the potatoes down with a spatula to baste periodically, until the gratin is nicely browned, about 30 minutes. (It's okay if the gratin is a little loose and creamy at this point.) Remove from the oven and let stand for 5 minutes before serving, to allow the gratin to settle and absorb some of the cream.

» Other sliced vegetables can be combined with the potatoes: turnips, celery root, leeks, winter squash, mushrooms, as well as wilted leafy greens between the layers. Apply the same method to other vegetable gratins without potatoes.

JEAN-PIERRE MOULLÉ has been a chef at Chez Panisse for nearly thirty years. He now spends six months as chef and the other six months in his native Bordeaux. When he first arrived at our kitchen in 1976, he had already trained and apprenticed in France, and he brought us culinary skill and a quiet seriousness of purpose. Jean-Pierre grew up hunting, fishing, and foraging and has never lost his love for the wild gifts of the land and sea.

« FILLETING A FISH »

Choose a very fresh whole fish and have your fish merchant gut and scale it and remove the gills. If you have one, a long, thin, sharp knife with a flexible blade is the best choice for filleting fish. Lay the fish on one side and make a cut behind the head and pectoral fin, but leave the head attached to the spine. Make another cut along the dorsal fin from the head to the tail. Insert the knife at about the center of the fish, and slice through the fish horizontally with the knife moving along the top of the spine and out toward the tail. Insert the knife again midway where you began, and cut along the spine moving back toward the head. Lift and remove the fillet and trim away any remaining flesh or small bones that were surrounding the gut cavity. Flip the fish over and repeat the process on the other side.

Depending on the type of fish and how you intend to cook it, you may want to remove the skin. To remove it, lay the fillet, skin side down, on the table with the tail end closest to you. Make a horizontal cut between the skin and the flesh at the tail end, freeing an inch or two of the skin. Grasp the skin tightly as you push the knife away from you, cutting horizontally between flesh and skin from one end to the other. Angle the blade down slightly, toward the skin. It is almost a scraping movement of the knife against the skin. Rinse the fillets and pat dry, and refrigerate or keep on ice until ready to cook.

FISH SOUP
4 SERVINGS

This is Jean-Pierre's simple and adaptable fish soup, which is a satisfying and economical way to cook and enjoy a whole fish. First fillet the fish, and then make a stock with the bones, vegetables, and herbs. Strain the stock and gently poach the fillets in it, then serve with croutons and pungent garlicky mayonnaise.

One 2- to 3-pound whole fish
   (firm white-fleshed such as
   rockfish, snapper, and ling cod)
1 small leek, white part only,
   sliced and rinsed
1 small onion, peeled and sliced
1 small carrot, peeled and sliced
A few black peppercorns
1 bay leaf

2 or 3 thyme sprigs
A few sprigs Italian parsley
1 cup dry white wine
6 cups cold water
Salt
4 slices crusty bread
Olive oil
Fresh-ground black pepper
Garlic Mayonnaise (page 27)

Fillet the fish, remove the skin, and refrigerate until ready to cook. Rinse the fish carcass and put it in a heavy pot. Add all the vegetables, the peppercorns, and herbs, cover with the wine and water, and add a good pinch of salt. Bring to a boil, then immediately lower the heat to a gentle simmer. Skim off any foam that rises to the surface. Simmer for 45 minutes, then strain the stock through a fine sieve. If you like, save some of the leek and carrot to add back to the strained stock.

Moisten the slices of bread with olive oil and toast in a 375°F oven for 10 minutes or so, until the croutons are browned and crisp. Pour the strained stock into a heavy pot and bring to a simmer. Cut the fillets into 2- to 3-inch pieces, season with salt and black pepper, and add to the stock. Poach the fish gently for 7 minutes or so, until just cooked through. Have warm soup bowls ready, and as soon as the fish is cooked, ladle the fish and stock into the bowls. Garnish with the croutons and Garlic Mayonnaise and serve. Pass more mayonnaise at the table.

» Shellfish, such as small clams and mussels, washed and beards removed, can be cooked along with the fish in the strained stock.
» The addition of potatoes, peeled and sliced, makes a more substantial soup. Cook them separately in salted water and add along with the fish, or simmer in the stock before adding the fish; they will take longer to cook than the fillets.
» Sweet ripe tomatoes, peeled (see page 53), seeded, and diced, make a delicious addition in the summer. A garnish of chopped tender herbs, such as parsley, chervil, marjoram, and basil adds brightness and freshness.

BAKED ROCKFISH WITH LEMON & PARSLEY BUTTER

4 SERVINGS

1 lemon
10 to 12 sprigs Italian parsley
1 shallot
6 tablespoons (¾ stick) butter
Salt and fresh-ground black pepper

Olive oil
1 to 1½ pounds rockfish fillets
  (or other fish; 4 to 6 ounces
  per serving)

First make the lemon and parsley butter. Grate the zest of the lemon. Chop the leaves of the parsley. Peel and finely dice the shallot, put it in a bowl, and squeeze lemon juice over to just cover. Let the shallot macerate in the juice for 10 minutes, then add the butter, lemon zest, and parsley. Season with salt and a generous amount of black pepper, and mash the butter to mix everything together.

Preheat the oven to 425°F. Lightly oil a shallow baking dish or roasting pan, or line with parchment paper. Place the fillets in the baking dish, season with salt and pepper, and moisten lightly with olive oil. Bake the fish for 7 to 10 minutes, depending on the thickness of the fillets, until just cooked through but still moist. Serve with a spoonful of the parsley butter on top of each fillet.

» Make the butter with another herb or combination of herbs (basil, chervil, chives, fennel, tarragon). If you like anchovies, add 3 or 4 chopped salt-packed anchovy fillets to the butter.
» Season and oil the fillets and wrap in fig leaves, grape leaves, or fennel branches for added flavor and to keep them moist while baking.
» Bake a whole fish at 375°F; it will take longer than fillets. If you like, make several diagonal cuts through the flesh to the bone for faster cooking. Season the fish and stuff the cavity of the fish with fresh herbs. If you have access to large branches of fennel or other herbs, wrap the whole fish in the branches and tie them closed before baking.

THOMAS KELLER is among the few chefs in the world who are at the very pinnacle of their profession. Comparing his restaurants to mine is a little like comparing Chartres Cathedral to a rustic chapel in the woods. But we hold a doctrine in common: a conviction that the quality of ingredients is everything in cooking. At home, Thomas cooks very simply, but with the same sensibility as at Per Se in New York, and the French Laundry in Napa Valley.

« ROASTING A CHICKEN »

Thomas likes to roast chicken and vegetables together in what he calls one-pot cooking. The vegetables make a bed for the chicken and prop it up so that it browns nicely, and the juices from the roasting bird permeate through the vegetables that caramelize on the bottom of the pot. He also removes the wishbone before cooking to make carving the roasted bird easier.

ONE-POT ROAST CHICKEN
4 SERVINGS

One 3-pound chicken
Salt and fresh-ground black pepper
3 potatoes, peeled and thickly sliced
2 carrots, peeled and thickly sliced
2 onions, peeled and quartered
2 celery stalks, thickly sliced

4 large shallots, peeled
Fennel, squash, turnips, parsnips,
  or other vegetables (optional)
2 bay leaves
2 or 3 thyme sprigs
2 to 3 tablespoons butter

First prepare the chicken. To remove the wishbone at the top of the breast, use a small knife to scrape along the bone to expose it, then insert the knife and run it along the bone, separating it from the flesh. Use your fingers to loosen it further, grasp the tip of the wishbone, and pull it out. Tuck the wing tips back and under the neck.

Tying the chicken plumps the breast up and brings the legs into position for even roasting. Cut a length of cotton string. With the chicken on its back, slip the string under the tail and bring the ends up over the legs to form a figure eight. Loop over the end of each leg and draw the string tight to bring the legs together. Draw the string back under the legs and wings on either side of the neck. Pull tight, wrap one end around the neck, and tie off the two ends. Salt the chicken evenly all around. Coarse salt has a good texture of large grains that makes it easy to calibrate how much salt you're putting on the chicken; sprinkle it from up high, so that it falls like snow. Season liberally with fresh-ground pepper.

Preheat the oven to 375°F, put all the vegetables and herbs together in the bottom of a large, heavy ovenproof pot, and season with salt and pepper. Set the chicken on top, dot with the butter, and roast uncovered for 45 to 60 minutes (or longer), depending on the size of the chicken. It is done when the leg joint is pierced with a knife and the juices run clear, not pink.

Let the chicken rest for a few minutes before carving (see page 109), and serve family-style with all the caramelized vegetables and juices from the pot on a platter and the chicken pieces on top.

ROAST CHICKEN
4 TO 6 SERVINGS

I like to roast a chicken with nothing more than a few herbs and seasonings. It is always satisfying, and the pan juices make a perfect sauce for the cooked bird.

One 3- to 4-pound chicken
Salt and fresh-ground pepper
Sprigs of thyme or other herbs
Olive oil

A day or two ahead of cooking, if possible, remove the neck and giblets from the chicken. If there are any lumps of fat just inside the cavity, pull them out and discard. Season the chicken inside and out with salt and fresh-ground pepper. Put a few sprigs of thyme or other herbs in the cavity, and truss, or tie, the legs together (see page 105 for tying instructions). Tuck the wing tips up and under the back of the neck. Cover loosely and refrigerate.

Remove the chicken from the refrigerator 1 hour before cooking and preheat the oven to 400°F. Place the chicken in a lightly oiled roasting pan or earthenware dish, breast side up. Roast for 20 minutes, then turn the chicken over, and roast breast side down, for another 20 minutes. Turn the chicken over again, and roast breast side up, for 20 minutes more. To test for doneness, pierce the leg joint with the tip of a knife; the juice should run clear, not pink. Remove the chicken to a platter to rest for 10 to 15 minutes before carving.

While the chicken is resting, prepare the pan juices. Tilt the pan to one corner and skim off much of the clear fat from the top. Put the pan on the stovetop, add a little chicken stock or water, and scrape loose all the browned bits on the bottom. When carving the chicken (see page 109), collect all the juice released from the bird and add to the pan juice. Heat the juices and pour over the chicken just before serving, or pass in a bowl at the table.

» The remains of roast chicken, and the flesh left on the carcass after carving, are good shredded and added to salads or mixed with an herb mayonnaise for chicken salad sandwiches, or added to a broth and vegetable soup (see page 48).
» Save the carcass of roast chicken for making stock. If the chicken has been roasted with fresh herbs in the cavity, remove them before adding the chicken to the stockpot.

CARVING A CHICKEN

Let the roasted chicken rest for 10 minutes or so after it is cooked. To carve the chicken, first cut the string and remove it. Cut off the legs: With the chicken on its back, use your fingers to push apart the leg and the breast and, with the knife, cut through the skin between the leg and the breast, following the seam down to the joint. Cut through the joint to release the ball of the leg bone from the socket and cut through the remaining attached skin. Repeat with the other leg.

Remove the breasts: Locate the breastbone at the center of the breast and cut straight down each side of it to the rib bones. With the wishbone removed, this is an easy, clean cut. If the wishbone has not been removed, use the tip of the knife and follow the wishbone down to the wing joint to separate the flesh from the bone. Use the knife to follow the rib bones down to the shoulder joint as you lift the breast away from the carcass, then cut through the wing joint, which will release very easily. If you like, cut the quarters into smaller pieces, separating legs and thighs, and cutting the breasts diagonally in half, or in slices.

JOYCE GOLDSTEIN was an early chef of the Chez Panisse Café. She has also been a groundbreaking cooking teacher, a prolific cookbook author, and the proprietor of her own restaurant in San Francisco, Square One, which was both a popular and a critical success. Her knowledge of—and passion for—foods from all around the Mediterranean is profound and inextinguishable.

« BRAISING »

Braising and stewing are methods of cooking gently and slowly in liquid with aromatic vegetables, herbs, and spices. Braised meats require long cooking, vegetables considerably less time.

MOROCCAN-STYLE BRAISED VEGETABLES
6 SERVINGS

This is a spicy and aromatic stew of chickpeas and tender vegetables. It is delicious served with pita bread, Buttered Couscous (page 79) or Saffron Rice (page 62), and spicy harissa sauce (see page 112).

For the chickpeas:
½ pound (1 cup) dried chickpeas, picked over and soaked overnight
1 small onion, peeled and halved
½ cinnamon stick
1 small dried red chile
2 tablespoons olive oil
Salt

Drain the chickpeas, put them in a medium pot, and add water to cover by 1½ inches. Add the onion, cinnamon stick, chile, olive oil, and a generous pinch of salt. Bring to a boil, reduce the heat to maintain a simmer, and cook gently until the chickpeas are tender, about 45 minutes. Taste for salt. Remove from the heat and allow the chickpeas to cool in the cooking liquid.

For the braised vegetables:
Salt
½ pound carrots
1 pound baby turnips
1½ pounds butternut squash
4 tablespoons olive oil
1 teaspoon cumin seeds
1 teaspoon coriander seeds
A pinch of saffron threads
½ teaspoon ground turmeric
⅛ teaspoon cayenne pepper
1 large onion, peeled and diced
2 celery stalks, diced
One 14-ounce can whole tomatoes
2 cloves garlic, peeled and chopped
1 teaspoon finely grated fresh ginger

Preheat the oven to 400°F. Bring a large pot of water to a boil and season with a generous amount of salt. Peel and halve the carrots and cut on the diagonal into 1-inch segments. Trim the turnips and cut into halves or quarters. Cook the carrots and turnips in separate batches until just tender, about 5 minutes. Spread the vegetables on a baking sheet to cool at room temperature.

(continued)

Peel and seed the squash, and cut into 1-inch chunks. Put the squash on a baking sheet, drizzle with 1 tablespoon of the olive oil, and toss to coat evenly. Spread the squash out to an even layer, season with salt, and roast in the oven until tender, 15 to 20 minutes. Set aside at room temperature.

Lightly toast the cumin seeds, coriander seeds, and saffron, and grind to a powder with a mortar and pestle or in a spice grinder. Add the turmeric and cayenne, and stir to combine.

Warm a large straight-sided skillet over medium heat. Add the remaining 3 tablespoons olive oil, followed by the onion, celery, and a pinch of salt. Cook for 5 minutes, stirring occasionally. Drain the tomatoes and cut into ¼-inch dice. Add the tomatoes to the skillet and cook for 2 minutes or until the vegetables are tender. Add the spices, garlic, and ginger, and cook for 2 minutes more. Add the chickpeas and the cooking liquid, and bring to a simmer. Add the squash, carrots, and turnips. At this point, there should be a nice amount of broth in the pan—like a chunky soup. If not, add water as necessary. Taste for salt, and simmer for 5 minutes. Serve with Buttered Couscous or Saffron Rice, and pass a bowl of harissa at the table.

» To make harissa: Toast 5 dried ancho chiles on a hot griddle until puffed and fragrant. Put the chiles in a bowl, cover with boiling water, soak for 20 minutes, and drain. Roast, peel, and seed 1 large red bell pepper (see page 85). In a blender or food processor, purée the drained chiles and peeled pepper with 4 peeled garlic cloves, ¾ cup olive oil, 1 teaspoon red wine vinegar, and salt to taste. Thin with water if desired.

BRAISED PORK SHOULDER
6 TO 8 SERVINGS

A shoulder roast of pork, lamb, or beef is ideal for braising; the shoulder is an economical cut with lots of flavor, and long, slow cooking yields succulent meat and a deep savory sauce. A braised shoulder is delicious accompanied by soft polenta, mashed potatoes, egg noodles, or creamy beans to soak up the tasty juices.

A roast with the bone in will hold together better during cooking and have more flavor. If the meat is boneless, it is helpful to tie it after seasoning. The braise will taste even better if seasoned a day before cooking and braised a day before serving.

One 4-pound bone-in pork shoulder roast

Salt and fresh-ground black pepper

1 to 2 tablespoons chopped sage or marjoram

1 onion, peeled and coarsely chopped

1 carrot, peeled and coarsely chopped

1 celery stalk, coarsely chopped

4 garlic cloves, peeled and chopped

2 bay leaves

2 cups chicken stock (page 47) or water

Gremolata (see page 17)

If it hasn't been trimmed already, remove any excess fat from the outside of the roast. Season the roast (if possible, a few hours ahead or the day before) with about 1 tablespoon salt, fresh-ground black pepper, and sage; rub the seasonings into the meat.

Bring the meat to room temperature if it has been refrigerated and preheat the oven to 375°F. Choose a heavy roasting pan or baking dish that will just hold the vegetables and roast. Put the vegetables and bay leaves in the pan, place the meat on top, and pour in the stock or water, which should come a quarter to a third of the way up the sides of the roast. Cook in the oven for 1 hour and 15 minutes. Turn the roast over and cook for another 30 minutes. Turn the roast again and return to the oven for 30 minutes more. Turning the meat allows it to alternately roast in the dry heat of the oven and stew in the simmering juices, which develops delicious flavors and textures. Check the level of the liquid during the cooking and add more if needed to maintain a consistent level. Cooking time will be 2½ to 3 hours; when done, the meat should be fork-tender and almost falling off the bone and should offer little or no resistance when poked with a skewer or knife.

Carefully remove the shoulder from the pan and let it rest at room temperature. Strain the sauce and skim well to remove the fat. Either discard the vegetables or push them through the strainer or pass them through a food mill and add them to the skimmed juices for a thicker, sweeter sauce. Taste the sauce and, if necessary, add salt and perhaps a splash of sweet vinegar. When the shoulder is cool enough to handle, remove the bones and cut the meat into thick slices. If it is to be served right away, gently reheat the sauce and meat; if not, refrigerate it in the pan and when ready to serve, reheat in the oven until the meat is just heated through. Serve the meat sprinkled generously with gremolata or freshly chopped herbs.

» Add dried chile or other spices to the braise, and, if you like, 2 or 3 chopped tomatoes or ½ cup white or red wine.

Moroccan-Style Braised Vegetables, page 111.

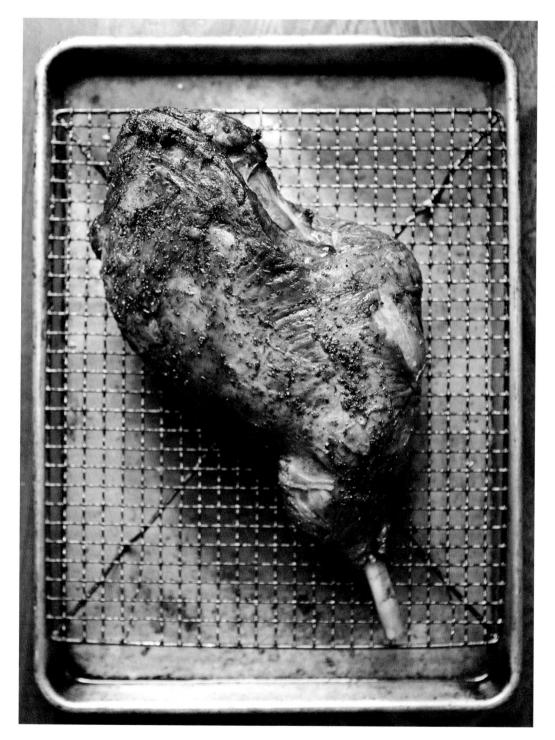

Roast Leg of Lamb, page 117.

PAUL BERTOLLI had a long career as a chef, at Chez Panisse and at his own restaurant, Oliveto. After writing two distinctive cookbooks, he turned his formidable intelligence to traditional Italian cured meats, opening his own *salumeria,* Fra' Mani, in Berkeley, California. He is an eloquent proponent of doing everything by hand, from scratch, and his sausages and hams are crafted in, as he puts it, "the Italian pastoral traditions."

« ROASTING MEAT »

The most important part of roasting is selecting the right meat. The best comes from animals that are pasture-raised, organically fed, hormone- and antibiotic-free, and, in many cases, locally produced. It will cost more than meat from factory farms, but that price translates into better stewardship of the land, better health and care for the animals, and tastier and healthier meat for us.

ROAST LEG OF LAMB
8 TO 10 SERVINGS

Leg of lamb cooks well either on the bone or boned. The price per pound will be more when boned, but the advantage is that it makes it very easy to slice and carve for serving. Have it tied by the butcher, or do it yourself at home. Roast lamb is traditionally served with beans, such as green flageolet or cannellini, and for a very good reason: They are a perfect combination.

1 leg of lamb (5 to 7 pounds)
Salt and fresh-ground black pepper
Rosemary or thyme, and garlic (optional)

Trim any excess fat from the leg of lamb, leaving a very thin layer. Season the roast liberally with salt and pepper, and, if you like, with chopped herbs; if time allows, do this one or two days before roasting. If the leg is boned and not yet tied, season it inside as well and add slices of garlic before tying with string (see page 118).

Remove the roast from the refrigerator at least 2 hours before cooking and put it in a roasting pan. If you like, put the meat on a bed of rosemary or woody thyme branches to perfume the roast while cooking. Roast the lamb in a preheated 375°F oven for 30 minutes, turn it over, and cook it for another 20 minutes. Turn it again and continue roasting until the internal temperature registers 128°F (medium-rare) on a meat thermometer. Take the reading at the center of the roast, the thickest and least-done part, without touching the bone. The total cooking time will be about 1 hour and 20 minutes, but start checking with the thermometer after an hour to make sure it is not overcooking. For meat cooked beyond medium-rare, to medium, take the roast out when it reaches 138°F. Let it rest in a warm place for 20 minutes before carving and serving.

Skim off the fat from the pan juices. Add a splash of wine, water, or stock to the pan and heat on the stove, scraping up all the browned bits on the bottom of the pan. Collect all the juices released from the meat after resting and carving, and add to the pan. Simmer briefly and serve with the meat.

Tying a Roast

Tying a roast, whether bone-in or boneless, will hold the meat together in one piece while roasting or braising, ensuring even cooking and integrity of shape and texture. It is best to season and flavor the meat before tying it.

Lay the roast on the table, lengthwise perpendicular to you. Stretch cotton string taut between your hands and slip it under the end of the roast nearest to you. Encircle the roast tightly about an inch from and parallel to the end, and tie a simple knot on the top. Hold the string up in one hand, then wrap it over the fingers of your other hand, spreading your fingers to make an open loop. Slip the loop over the front end of the roast and drag it back to about an inch in front of and parallel to the first tied loop, and give the string a tug to tighten it. Hold the string taut to keep it tight around the roast and repeat: Make another loop, slip it under the front of the roast, drag it down to the previous one, and pull it tight; proceed several more times to nearly the end of the roast.

Continue to keep tension on the string, pull it under the end of the roast, and turn the roast over. Pull the string back to you, about twice the length of the roast, and cut it. Then make a series of half hitches around each loop: Starting with the far end, lift up the loop, slip the string under and around it, and pull it snug. Do the same for the next loop, and so on, down to the last one at the end nearest you. Flip the roast over, pull the string up over the end, and tie it off at the knot of the first loop, the starting point. Trim the string ends, and done.

Pork Rib Roast with Rosemary & Sage
4 to 6 servings

A bone-in pork rib roast has everything: lean and moist meat, a crusty fatty exterior, and rib bones. When you buy the roast, ask the butcher to remove the spinal chine bone and to separate the thin layer of meat on the ribs, stopping about an inch from the end of the bones. This allows you to season the interior of the meat next to the bones. Season the meat 1 or 2 days before cooking; it makes a big difference in the flavor of the roast.

1 bone-in 4- or 5-rib pork loin
3 garlic cloves, peeled and chopped
Salt and fresh-ground black pepper

1 tablespoon chopped rosemary
1 tablespoon chopped sage leaves

Open the flap of meat next to the rib bones and rub the garlic onto the meat and bones down to the loin meat. Sprinkle liberally with salt, ground pepper, and half the rosemary and sage. Rub the seasonings into the meat. Reassemble the roast and use kitchen string to tie the meat and bones together. Season the outside of the roast, again liberally, with salt, pepper, and the remaining herbs, and rub into the meat. The chopped garlic goes on the inside of the roast; if rubbed onto the outside, it will burn in the oven. Wrap up the roast in the butcher paper, or lightly cover, and refrigerate.

Remove the roast from the refrigerator an hour or so before cooking to let it come to room temperature. Put it in a roasting pan, bone side down; the bones make a sort of natural roasting rack. Preheat the oven to 400°F. Cook the roast for 30 minutes or so, then turn it over in the roasting pan, bone side up, and cook for another 20 minutes. Turn the roast again, bone side down, and cook another 20 minutes or so, until the internal temperature registers 130°F. When the roast is done, let it rest for 15 to 20 minutes before carving.

Skim off some of the fat from the roasting pan, add some water or stock, and scrape up all the browned bits on the bottom of the pan. Pour the juices into a small saucepan and keep warm. When ready to serve, remove the strings from the roast, and cut the meat into thick chops with the bones, or cut the rack of rib bones away from the meat, and slice between the bones to separate them. Return them to the oven for a few minutes if you like them crustier. To the juices in the saucepan, add the juices released from the roast after resting and carving. Slice the meat and serve with the warm juices and the rib bones.

PEGGY KNICKERBOCKER describes herself as a Francophile and a freelance travel and food writer, but she is no mere dilettante: She is a fierce and articulate advocate of home cooking, farmers' markets, and good olive oil. Her books (of which the most recent is *The San Francisco Ferry Plaza Farmers' Market Cookbook,* co-authored with Christopher Hirsheimer) and her teaching have won awards and changed lives; her cooking is exuberant, wide-eyed, and full of energy.

« GRILLING A STEAK »

I don't cook steak very often; but when I do, I choose grass-fed, organically raised beef and cook it on a grill over a wood or charcoal fire. A fine cut for steak is rib eye on the bone; a rib eye steak that is 2 to 2½ inches thick will grill beautifully, crusty on the outside and pink and juicy on the inside, and there will be plenty of meat for two servings. Porterhouse steak is another substantial cut that serves two. For serving more people, try such flavorful, less expensive cuts as hanger steak, skirt steak, sirloin, and flatiron chuck steak. Individual fillet or tenderloin steaks are the most tender.

GRILLED FILLET STEAK WITH HERBS
2 SERVINGS

Two 5- to 6-ounce fillet steaks, cut about 2 inches thick
Olive oil
Salt
Fresh-ground black pepper

¼ cup mixed chopped herbs: rosemary, thyme, marjoram, savory, and oregano
2 garlic cloves, peeled and finely chopped (optional)

Rub the steaks lightly with olive oil, season with salt and fresh-ground pepper, and coat them generously with chopped fresh herbs. You can do this a few hours or a day ahead of time. Let the steak come to room temperature at least 30 minutes before cooking,

Prepare a fire with wood or wood charcoal and let it burn down to a thick bed of hot coals. The grill should be very hot and brushed clean before you put the steaks on. How long to cook the meat depends on its thickness and how hot the fire is. A 2-inch fillet steak will take 6 to 8 minutes on one side, and 4 to 8 minutes on the other, depending on how rare you like it. If the fire flares up, move the steaks to a cooler part of the grill briefly before returning them to a hot spot. Test for doneness by pressing with your finger; the meat will be soft when rare, springy when medium-rare, and firm when well done. Cut into the meat to check if you are unsure. When they are done to your liking, remove the steaks and let them rest for several minutes for the juices to stabilize before serving. For added flavor, while they are still hot from the grill, sprinkle the steaks with finely chopped garlic.

CLAIRE PTAK is an intractable idealist in the kitchen and a perfectionist after my own heart. She was a pastry chef at Chez Panisse before she moved to London, where she opened what she describes as "a little cake business," a market stall called Violet Cakes, where she sells the purest, simplest desserts imaginable. In the kitchen, her meticulousness, gracefulness, and attention to detail remind me of an Olympic gymnast.

« BAKING FRUIT »

I love fruit at the end of a meal and am easily satisfied with whatever is ripe and in season. However, if I have guests and want to give them something more than fresh fruit, simply baking sweet peaches or nectarines transforms them into a warm and fragrant dessert. All kinds of fruits are lovely baked—pears, nectarines, apricots, pluots, apples—but peaches are particularly luscious and juicy. This recipe gilds the lily a bit with berries and wine. If those ingredients are not on hand, don't let that stop you; the peaches are wonderful baked without them.

BAKED PEACHES
4 SERVINGS

4 ripe freestone peaches
1 cup huckleberries, blackberries,
   or raspberries (optional)
3 to 4 tablespoons sugar

½ cup white wine, Beaumes-de-Venise
   or other dessert wine, or water
Whipped cream or vanilla ice cream
(optional)

Preheat the oven to 375°F. Halve the peaches and remove the pits. Arrange the peaches in a shallow gratin dish, cut-side up, in a snug single layer. If you like, fill the cavity of each peach with berries. Sprinkle the sugar over the peaches and berries—more or less, depending on the fruits' sweetness. Drizzle the wine or water over the fruit. Bake the peaches for about 20 minutes, until juicy and tender. Serve warm with their juices and, if you like, with softly whipped cream or vanilla ice cream.

» If you prefer, peel the peaches before baking: Drop the peaches in boiling water for 20 seconds or so, just enough to loosen the skins. Lift them out and plunge immediately into ice water. When cool, slip off the skins.
» In place of the berries, the peaches are delicious baked with an almond stuffing: Cream together ¼ cup butter and 1 tablespoon sugar. Blend in 1 small egg yolk, ¼ cup lightly toasted and chopped almonds, and 4 crushed macaroon cookies. Spoon the stuffing into the cavities of the peaches and bake. The stuffing is equally good with pears, nectarines, or apricots.

APPLE GALETTE
6 TO 8 SERVINGS

If I'm going to make a fruit tart or pie, it is most often a galette—a thin, free-form open-face tart. The pastry is easy to make and roll out, and is crisp and light when baked. The dough is not sweet and can be used for savory tarts as well as dessert.

This recipe makes enough dough for 2 tarts. The dough will keep in the refrigerator for 2 days or in the freezer for several months.

2 cups unbleached all-purpose flour
½ teaspoon salt
   (omit if using salted butter)
12 tablespoons (1½ sticks) cold
   unsalted butter
⅓ to ½ cup ice-cold water

4 or 5 medium apples
   (Sierra Beauty, Gravenstein, or
   any flavorful variety)
Sugar
1 egg
Whipped cream (optional)

Measure the flour and salt (if including) into a bowl. The butter should be cold and firm, but not hard. Cut it into ¼- to ½-inch cubes and put about half of it into the bowl. Work it into the flour with your fingertips, lightly rubbing and breaking the flour-coated pieces of butter into small bits, until the mixture is roughly the texture of oatmeal or cornmeal. Add the rest of the butter and work it quickly into the dough until the pieces of butter are about half their original size. Dribble the water into the dough while tossing the mixture with a fork. Keep adding water only until the dough begins to clump and hold together when you squeeze a handful. You may not need the full ½ cup. Divide the dough in two and gather each part into a ball. Wrap each ball in plastic and flatten it into a disk. Let the dough rest, refrigerated, for an hour or so. You may want to freeze the second disk of dough for future use.

When ready to make the tart, let the dough warm up at room temperature for 15 minutes or so and preheat the oven to 400°F. Roll out the dough on a lightly floured surface into a rough circle about 12 inches in diameter and about ⅛ inch thick. Transfer the pastry to a baking sheet lined with parchment paper and refrigerate while preparing the apples.

Peel, core, and slice the apples and toss with 1 to 2 tablespoons of sugar. Arrange the apples on the pastry, in overlapping concentric circles or freely piled on top, however you like, but leaving a 1½-inch border of dough around the whole circumference. Fold the dough up over the apples, and brush the rim of dough lightly with beaten egg. Sprinkle sugar over the dough and apples; use more or less, depending on the tartness of the apples. Bake in the lower part of the oven for 45 to 50 minutes, until the fruit is tender and the pastry is golden brown and slightly caramelized at the edges. Slide the tart off the pan to cool on a rack. Serve warm or at room temperature—with softly whipped cream, if you like.

» Juicy stone fruits such as peaches, nectarines, apricots, and plums make wonderful galettes. To help absorb the juices and keep the pastry bottom crisp, sprinkle a mixture of 2 tablespoons sugar, 1 tablespoon flour, and 1 tablespoon ground almonds on the pastry before topping with fruit.
» Apple galette is delicious when you spread the rolled-out dough with homemade apricot jam before arranging the apples on top. After baking, brush the apples with warm apricot jam for a beautiful glaze.

Nectarine & Berry Cobbler
10 SERVINGS

Cobblers are mostly fruit, with the sweet cobbler biscuits floating on top to soak up all the juices. They are a good thing to make when you have an abundance of fruit and a number of people to cook for. Make them all year round with whatever ripe fruits are in season, either singly or in combination. They are superb served warm for dessert but even better for breakfast the next morning.

½ recipe Sweet Cream Biscuits
   (page 34)
5 cups sliced nectarines
   (¼-inch slices)
2 cups blueberries
2 cups blackberries
¾ cup sugar

¼ cup unbleached all-purpose flour
A pinch of salt
Zest of 1 lemon
¼ cup lemon juice
¼ cup whipping cream
Vanilla ice cream or whipped cream
   (optional)

Prepare half the Sweet Cream Biscuits recipe on page 34. Cut out 10 biscuits using a 2½-inch round cutter, or 14 biscuits with a 2-inch cutter. A cutter with scalloped edges makes beautiful cobbler biscuits.

Preheat the oven to 400°F. Combine the fruit in a large bowl. Mix ½ cup sugar, flour, and salt together, and stir into the fruit. Add the lemon zest and juice, and mix well. Put the fruit in a gratin dish approximately 9 inches by 12 inches and 2 to 3 inches deep. Bake the fruit for 8 minutes or until the fruit just softens. Remove the dish from the oven. Brush the biscuit tops with the cream and sprinkle lightly with the remaining sugar. Place the biscuits on the fruit in staggered rows and return the dish to the oven (set the dish on a baking sheet to catch any overflowing juices). Bake the cobbler for 35 to 45 minutes, until the biscuits are golden and the fruit is bubbling. Let the cobbler cool awhile and serve warm with vanilla ice cream or lightly whipped cream, if you like.

» Use other stone fruit in place of the nectarines; plums will need 1 to 2 tablespoons additional sugar, and the slices should be slightly thinner. Use all nectarines, or peaches or other stone fruit, if berries are not available.

» Instead of cobbler biscuits, bake the fruit with a crisp topping: Mix together 1¼ cups flour, 6 tablespoons brown sugar, 1½ tablespoons granulated sugar, ¼ teaspoon ground cinnamon, and ⅔ cup lightly toasted chopped nuts (walnuts, pecans, or almonds). Work in 12 tablespoons butter cut into small pieces until the mixture has a crumbly texture. Cover the fruit in the pan with the crisp topping and bake until the fruit is bubbling thickly and the topping is lightly browned.

Clockwise from upper left: King, Gravenstein, and Jonathan apples; Charentais melon; Concord and Bronx grapes; Autumn Flame peach; Seascape strawberries; Seckel pears; pineapple quince; O'Henry peach; French butter pear; Greek Royal, Mission, and Turkey figs; Elsa's Choice raspberries; Emerald Beaut plum.

Murray River salt from Australia.

« SEASONING FOR FLAVOR »

Salt is key to bringing out the flavor of most foods, and it's good to have a few kinds on hand for different purposes: coarse sea salt or additive-free kosher salt for general purposes, and finer sea salt for finishing dishes. Sea salt is produced by the evaporation of water from the brine of the sea. It is both milder than refined table salt and more flavorful because of the trace mineral content. Sea salts are sometimes gray or pink or other shades because of the minerals at the source. Flaky salts, such as Maldon and fleur de sel (flower of salt), have a delicate texture and flavor, and are delicious crushed between your fingers and added as a final seasoning. Maldon salt has a light flavor and lacy texture obtained by boiling the seawater before drying. Fleur de sel are crystals that are harvested by hand-raking the surface of seawater evaporation basins.

Coarse salt has a good feel in the hand. It is easy to apply with your fingertips and gives you a more accurate sense of how much you are using than shaking from a container. I keep a dish within easy reach of the stove to dip into. Season with salt at various stages of cooking, depending on the dish, and not just at the end. Chopped vegetables seasoned with salt and herbs and gently sautéed for the base of a soup or a stew build flavor into the whole dish. If you make each stage of a preparation taste good on its own, the end result should be delicious. Seasoning meat and poultry with coarse salt and pepper a day or two in advance of cooking makes an enormous difference in flavor because there is time for the salt to penetrate deeper than the surface of the meat.

Black, white, and green peppercorns are all fruit of the same vine. The differences in color and flavor result from the peppercorns having been harvested at different stages of their development and from the ways they are processed. Black pepper has the strongest, most pungent flavor. Tellicherry and Lampong black peppercorns are especially good. White pepper is milder and less pungent. Pepper is best ground fresh because the fragrant oils that are an important component of its flavor are extremely volatile.

The flavors of spices are fleeting. I keep small quantities on hand and replenish them often. I usually have chile flakes and chile powder (including Marash red pepper and cayenne), saffron, bay leaves, nutmeg, ginger, cinnamon, cloves, and vanilla beans. Because seeds such as cumin, fennel, and coriander taste better freshly ground, buy them whole. Toasting just before use enlivens their

AMARYLL SCHWERTNER is the co-owner and chef of a remarkable business called Boulettes Larder in the San Francisco Ferry Building, which is both a working restaurant kitchen and a producer of foods to take home, including ingredients marinated for grilling; spice blends from North Africa, Turkey, and Greece; Japanese salts and sugars; condiments, both house-made and imported; delicious pastries; and much more.

flavor: Heat the seeds in a hot dry pan for a minute or so, until their aroma is released, cool briefly, and grind in a mortar.

Fresh herbs bring a fragrant vitality to the kitchen. I can't imagine cooking without any of these: parsley, basil, chives, marjoram, oregano, tarragon, thyme, chervil, cilantro, mint, rosemary, sage, and savory. With only a few exceptions, notably thyme and oregano, most dried herbs are bland substitutes for themselves, and not worth bothering with. Fresh herbs, on the other hand, are indispensable: branches tied up in bunches and used to flavor dishes that are roasting or simmering; leaves and flowers stripped off their stems and branches, freshly chopped, and scattered over a dish at the last minute; or the leaves of such herbs as rosemary, sage, parsley, and savory shallow-fried in olive oil for less than a minute, just until crisp, drained, and scattered over fried potatoes, pastas, roasted meats, or whatever you like.

I think of lemon as a seasoning, especially as a final adjustment to lift and brighten other flavors while balancing saltiness and the richness of butter or oil. Experiment. Taste what happens with the addition of a final squeeze of lemon juice to a salad or a soup. (Vinegar can work in a similar way.) Tasting and adjusting the balance of acid and salt is a key part of seasoning for maximum flavor.

Left to right: vanilla beans; top row: Marash pepper; ground cumin; curry; middle row: turmeric; pimentón; cinnamon; bottom row: saffron; coriander seeds; cumin seeds.

« COOKING EQUIPMENT »

I want to dispel the notion that you need a lot of specialized equipment to cook good food. All you need is a core group of pots and pans and tools that will do most anything. I have been given many fancy pans and gadgets and electrical appliances over the years, and invariably I find that they languish unused in the back of a cupboard for a time until I eventually pass them on. I tend to use the same reliable pans over and over. For me, it is a case of less is more, and form following function; the food that I like to cook and eat is uncomplicated and easily accomplished with simple equipment. That said, it is worthwhile investing in solid, well-made, heavy pans and quality knives that will literally last a lifetime. No one goes out and buys everything all at once, but with one addition at a time, you can build what the French call a *batterie de cuisine* that works for you in your kitchen for the food you like to cook. Here is a list of the equipment that I find essential and that I use most often.

Knives and cutting board
Compost bucket
Cast-iron skillets: 6, 10, and 12 inches
12-inch stainless steel–lined sauté pan
1-quart saucepan
2- to 3-quart stainless steel–lined saucepan with lid
3- to 4-gallon stockpot
4- to 6-quart ovenproof pot with a lid
Baking sheets and roasting pan
Earthenware and gratin dishes of various sizes
Steamer basket and sieves
Salad spinner and colander
Small food processor or blender, or spice grinder
Bowls of various sizes
Mortars and pestles of various sizes
Rolling pin, and tart and pie pans
A selection of small tools:
  wooden spoons, spatulas, whisks, tongs,
  pepper grinder, vegetable peeler, grater,
  measuring cups and spoons, corkscrew

KNIVES

The three essential knives are a paring knife, a chef's knife, and a bread knife. A paring knife with a short, narrow blade is for peeling and trimming fruits and vegetables and cutting small things. An 8- or 9-inch chef's knife, with a wedge-shaped blade wide at the heel near the handle and tapering to a point at the tip, is the most versatile knife in the kitchen. Japanese chef's knives are similarly shaped, less tapered and not as pointed at the tip; I find them to be excellent. A chef's knife is the workhorse tool for most chopping, dicing, and slicing. While it can be useful to have a few specialty knives for boning, filleting, and carving, a chef's knife will do these jobs, too. Finally, a bread knife with a long serrated blade is necessary for slicing bread (sawing, really), particularly crusty country-style breads.

Knives are worth the investment; it's better to have a few knives of high quality than an array of inferior ones. Choose knives with a high carbon steel content: They will sharpen well on a whetstone and maintain a sharp edge. They should feel well balanced and not too heavy, and the handles should fit comfortably in your hand. Keep knives sharp for best performance, and also for safety: Sharp knives are far safer than dull ones. With a stone and some instruction, you can learn to sharpen your knives yourself, or you can have them sharpened by someone who is skilled at the job. Between sharpenings with a stone, use a sharpening steel, a long, tapered hard-steel rod with a handle and a hand guard, to hone the knife's edge. Clean and dry your knives after each use, don't put them in the dishwasher, and store them in a way that protects the edge.

Chopping is a process of cutting ingredients into smaller and smaller pieces in an imprecise way. A rough chop means large pieces; a fine chop, very small ones. Mincing is chopping very fine, almost to a paste. I find that in most instances, it is easier and more efficient to dice ingredients—that is, to cut them into cubes—rather than chop them. To dice something, first cut it into slices, cut the slices into matchsticks, and cut the matchsticks into cubes.

To dice an onion, cut it in half lengthwise through the stem and root ends and peel off the skin. Trim off the stem end, but leave the root end intact. Put the halves on a cutting board, cut side down, and make a few horizontal cuts parallel to the board, starting at the stem end and cutting all the way to, but not through, the root end. Then make parallel vertical cuts straight down, again cutting to, but not through, the root end. (For a fine dice, make the cuts very close together; for a larger dice, make them farther apart.) Turn the onion and cut crosswise into dice. Discard the root end. Dicing is preferable to chopping for ingredients such as shallots for a vinaigrette, because it cuts without bruising and smashing, which releases the juices.

Diced vegetables (mirepoix), left to right: red onion; carrot; fennel; celery; finely chopped garlic.

« Friends & Cooks »

LEFT TO RIGHT:
Alice Waters
Fanny Singer, 10
Traci Des Jardins, 16
Joan Nathan, 20
Gilbert Pilgram, 22

LEFT TO RIGHT:
Rick Bayless, 24
Jérôme Waag, 26
Darina Allen, 30
Scott Peacock, 32
Clodagh McKenna, 36

LEFT TO RIGHT:
Angelo Garro, 42
Beth Wells, 46
Charlie Trotter, 52
Lidia Bastianich, 56
Poppy Tooker, 60

« ACKNOWLEDGMENTS »

I am most grateful to those enthusiastic and determined activists, organizers, cooks, producers, and co-producers who built Slow Food Nation (a project of Slow Food USA in San Francisco) from the ground up, and whose commitment to good, clean, and fair food inspired the live cooking demonstrations presented at The Green Kitchen.

The Green Kitchen would not have been possible without the indefatigable efforts of Carolyn Federman, Ed Acosta, Samantha Greenwood, Marsha Guerrero, Varun Mehra, Joyce Cellars, and our dedicated volunteers. Special thanks to Craig St. John and team for video production; to Liz Hasse for legal advice; to architects Hans Baldauf, Hannah Brown, and Casimiro Camacho; and to Davia Nelson and Sue Murphy for their gracious and witty commentary.

My utmost appreciation goes to the remarkable contributing friends and chefs, whom Christopher Hirsheimer and Melissa Hamilton so perfectly captured—their extraordinary photography made possible the creation of this book. I am grateful to my friend and literary agent, David McCormick; to artist Christina Kim, at dosa; and to my editor, Emily Takoudes.

As always, I am indebted to the collaborative brilliance of Patricia Curtan and Fritz Streiff.

« INDEX »